天津市鲁班工坊研究与推广中心成果

Research Results of Tianjin Luban Workshop Research and Promotion Center

LUBAN
WORKSHOP

鲁班工坊

发展蓝皮书(2023)(中英双语版)

BLUE BOOK OF THE DEVELOPMENT OF LUBAN
WORKSHOP (2023) (BILINGUAL EDITION IN
CHINESE AND ENGLISH)

杨延　　王岚　　王凤慧 ◎ 著
By Yang Yan, Wang Lan, Wang Fenghui

天津出版传媒集团

天津人民出版社

图书在版编目（CIP）数据

鲁班工坊发展蓝皮书.2023：汉英对照/杨延，王
岚，王凤慧著.-- 天津：天津人民出版社，2024.12.
ISBN 978-7-201-20987-6

Ⅰ.G719.2

中国国家版本馆 CIP 数据核字第 20255QC801 号

鲁班工坊发展蓝皮书（2023）（中英双语版）
LUBANGONGFANG FAZHAN LANPISHU（2023）（ZHONGYING SHUANGYU BAN）

出　　　版　天津人民出版社
出 版 人　刘锦泉
地　　　址　天津市和平区西康路 35 号康岳大厦
邮政编码　300051
邮购电话　（022）23332469
电子信箱　reader@tjrmcbs.com

责任编辑　王佳欢
封面设计　路炳川

印　　　刷　天津新华印务有限公司
经　　　销　新华书店
开　　　本　710 毫米×1000 毫米　1/16
印　　　张　5
插　　　页　2
字　　　数　80 千字
版次印次　2024 年 12 月第 1 版　2024 年 12 月第 1 次印刷
定　　　价　68.00 元

天津市鲁班工坊
研究与推广中心

鲁班工坊
LUBAN WORKSHOP

中文版

目录
CONTENTS

i

综　述

2023 年是"一带一路"倡议提出 10 周年。在第三届"一带一路"国际合作高峰论坛上，习近平主席提出，独具特色的鲁班工坊、"丝路一家亲"、"光明行"等人文交流项目，不断深化的民间组织、智库、媒体、青年交流，奏响新时代的丝路乐章。未来还将继续通过鲁班工坊等项目推进中外职业教育高水平合作。鲁班工坊已成为服务国家外交的金色名片。

截至 2023 年 12 月，中国已经在亚洲的泰国、印度、印度尼西亚、巴基斯坦、柬埔寨、塔吉克斯坦，欧洲的英国、葡萄牙、保加利亚、塞尔维亚、俄罗斯，非洲的吉布提、肯尼亚、南非、马里、尼日利亚、埃及、科特迪瓦、乌干达、马达加斯加、埃塞俄比亚、摩洛哥、卢旺达、加蓬、贝宁等国家创建了 29 个鲁班工坊。鲁班工坊已经建立了从中职到高职、应用本科，再到研究生层次的国际职业教育体系。

天津市鲁班工坊研究与推广中心不完全统计显示，目前在鲁班工坊国际合作专业注册的学历生和其他专业选修课程的学历生已达到 1.76 万人，项目合作的国际企业有 144 家。鲁班工坊的培训面向合作国当地企业员工，合作院校及区域院校的师生、社会人员等，累计培训总量为 9.54 万人次，为合作国经济社会发展培养了大量急需的技术技能人才，持续支持和促进合作国繁荣发展与中外深化合作，成为推动人类命运共同体建设的重要力量。

　　经过 7 年的积累，以鲁班工坊为载体中外合作共同推动职业教育的发展与进步，中外专业教师共同建设国际合作专业，开发教学资源，已公开出版双语教材 145 本，相关校本教材 420 本（含中外文自编实训讲义、实训工作手册等）。在泰国、印度尼西亚、巴基斯坦、印度、埃及、埃塞俄比亚、葡萄牙、肯尼亚、哈萨克斯坦、乌兹别克斯坦、马达加斯加、俄罗斯 12 个国家设立了 EPIP 研究推广中心，推广先进的教学理念与教学模式。鲁班工坊已累计为相关国家培训教师 3300 余人次，累计培训总时长约 20.32 万小时。

图 1　全球鲁班工坊分布图

第一章
建设发展进程与重大成果

一、汇聚多方力量，实现跨越发展

2023 年 5 月，天津召开鲁班工坊建设联盟第二次成员大会，这是鲁班工坊建设联盟扩容后的首次成员大会，300 余位联盟成员代表出席本次大会。其中，新增院校会员 140 所，企业会员 46 家。截至 2023 年，鲁班工坊建设联盟成员单位达到 323 个，包括 258 个成员单位（200 所院校成员单位、54 个企业及行业协会成员单位、4 所研究机构成员单位），以及 65 所院校观察员单位，实现了联盟网络跨越式发展。

联盟扩容为更多的中国院校、企业和研究机构参与鲁班工坊建设搭建起交流平台，第二次成员大会分设非洲专场，亚洲专场，欧洲、拉美、阿拉伯等地区专场，从全球不同区域职业教育国际合作探索出发，共同探讨鲁班工坊及境外办学项目建设经验、路径、特色及挑战应对。同时，借助联盟平台汇聚各方资源、形成强大合力，促进联盟成员单位统一认识、凝聚共识，为鲁班工坊这一境外办学品牌项目实现高标准定位、高水平建设、高质量发展提供前进动力。

成立鲁班工坊建设专家委员会。专委会由工科、职业教育、国际中文、行业企业等多领域专家组成，发挥专委会的专业优势，通过组织开展专业调研论证，对鲁班工坊建设提出专业性、建设性意见建议，为鲁班工坊高质量发展提供高水平专业咨询，提升鲁班工坊建设相关工作科学化水平。

二、助力对外开放，持续新建项目

推进鲁班工坊建设等职业教育合作项目列入中国-中亚峰会成果清单。2023 年 5 月，中国-中亚峰会提出实施"中国-中亚技术技能提升计划"，在中亚国家设立更多鲁班工坊，鼓励在中亚的中资企业为当地提供更多就业机会。

中国院校在中亚建设鲁班工坊进入快车道。2023 年 8 月，浙江水利水电学院、浙江交通职业技术学院与吉尔吉斯斯坦国立技术大学共同签署《中吉鲁班工坊合作备忘录》，标志着吉尔吉斯斯坦鲁班工坊进入实质性筹建阶段。2023 年 12 月，依据《鲁班工坊建设规程》《鲁班工坊运营项目认定标准（试行）》，按照认定工作程序，经中国教育国际交流协会与天津市教育委员会联合认定，并经鲁班工坊建设联盟理事会审议通过，天津职业大学与东哈萨克斯坦技术大学合作项目、天津海运职业学院与乌兹别克斯坦塔什干国立交通大学合作项目被认定为鲁班工坊运营项目。

三、强化产权保护，提升品牌价值

为加强鲁班工坊国际知识产权保护，2022 年 10 月，启动了英国鲁班工坊知识产权保护工作，经过严谨的准备，天津市教育科学研究院作为申请人于 2023 年正式向英国知识产权局提起商标权申请。在第 41 类产品服务类别上，鲁班工坊商标于 2023 年 7 月由英国知识产权局按照正常程序正式核准注册，明确鲁班工坊商标受到英国政府认可及英国商标法的保护，鲁班工坊商标在英国可以使用且受保护范围主要包括：教学、教育服务、学术讨论会的安排和组织、图书出版、竞赛组织（教育或娱乐）、以文化或教育目的组织展览、广播电视节目制作等诸多方面。

英国鲁班工坊商标权注册的意义重大，标志着具有中国知识产权的职教品牌项目在海外合作国获得法律保护，有力地提升了中国职教国际合作项目鲁班工坊的品牌价值。

四、试点质量评估，推动持续发展

对完成三年建设周期的鲁班工坊开展质量评估是确保项目高质量、可持续发展的制度保障。天津市鲁班工坊研究与推广中心组建专家组，基于天津院校建设鲁班工坊的成功经验，研究制定了试行版的《鲁班工坊质量评估指标体系》，从鲁班工坊的总体发展与项目建设成效等多个方面对鲁班工坊总体建设质量和发展能力进行综合性评价。质量评估试点工作在 2021 年启动，研推中心从鲁班工坊建设联盟和具有丰富国际合作理论与实践基础的全国专家中遴选组建专家团队，对项目进行系统化的质量评估，评估方式采取鲁班工坊研推中心独立第三方问卷调查评估、专家组质询、现场检查等多种形式，从不同视角对鲁班工坊进行综合性评价。

截至 2023 年底，已完成泰国鲁班工坊、英国鲁班工坊、印度尼西亚鲁班工坊、柬埔寨鲁班工坊、印度鲁班工坊、巴基斯坦鲁班工坊、葡萄牙鲁班工坊和吉布提鲁班工坊 8 个项目的质量评估试点工作。实践探索显示，质量评估对鲁班工坊持续发展的作用是显著的，不仅帮助项目组凝练特色创新经验，也为项目可持续发展指明了方向。

五、引领职教出海，荣获国家奖项

鲁班工坊作为中国职教出海的金色名片，其建设与发展凝聚了中国职业教育改革与发展的优秀成果。目前，鲁班工坊已经有两项成果获得国家级教学成果奖:《开发国际化专业教学标准，创设"鲁班工坊"职业教育国际合作的研究与实践》获得 2018 年国家级教学成果奖一等奖，为职业教育国际合作教育教学领域的深化改革探索路径。《模式创立、标准研制、资源开发、师资培养——鲁班工坊的创新实践》获得 2022 年国家级教学成果特等奖，这项成果解决了职业教育国际化的基础性问题：一是有效解决了职业教育国际合作长期存在的模式盲从、标准依赖、效果不彰等问题；二是系统解决了中国职教面向世界实施产教融合，开展跨国界职教合作的内涵依据问题；三是解决了中国职业教育走出去，与世界分享的路径、载体与保障问题。

第二章
项目内涵与基础能力提升

一、合作专业规模发展

随着鲁班工坊项目建设的发展，中外合作国际专业的规模不断扩大，到 2023 年累计开发了装备制造、电子信息、交通运输、土木建筑、能源动力与材料、财经商贸、旅游与医药卫生等 14 个大类共计 76 个专业，较 2022 年度增加 15%，其中以高职专业为主，占比达到 80%。

这些专业均紧紧围绕合作国家的经济转型和产业发展需求而开设。如基于埃及绿色经济与工业化发展的需求，创立了新能源应用技术、数控设备应用与维护、汽车运用与维修技术等专业；顺应高速铁路建设需求，在泰国、吉布提、尼日利亚开设铁路运维与相关管理专业；适应信息技术、智能技术发展需求，在南非、肯尼亚等国家开设物联网应用技术、云计算等专业……先进制造技术类专业是所有鲁班工坊建设的需求最大的专业类别，涉及葡萄牙、马达加斯加、印度、巴基斯坦、乌干达、科特迪瓦等国家，这也反映了当前各国发展对技术进步的需求。

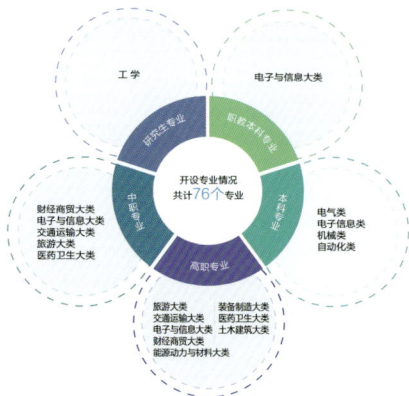

图 2　鲁班工坊建设专业情况

二、办学场地不断拓展

办学场地是鲁班工坊项目顺利进行的物质基础和关键载体。统计数据显示，鲁班工坊项目目前的办学场地总面积已超过 38000 平方米，较 2022 年度增加 3832 平方米，主要用于专业实习实训教学、基础实验课程、人文交流活动、项目成果展示，等等。

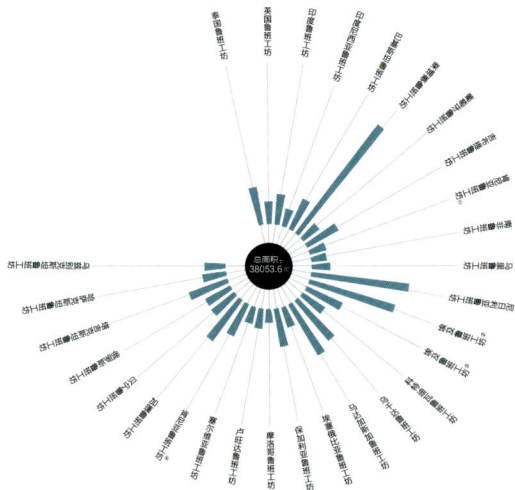

①为天津城市职业学院合作共建项目。
②与埃及艾因夏姆斯大学合作共建。
③与埃及开罗高级维修技术学校合作共建。
④为陕西铁路工程职业技术学院合作共建项目。

图 3　鲁班工坊场地建设情况

其中，12个鲁班工坊的场地面积超过1000平方米，柬埔寨鲁班工坊、尼日利亚鲁班工坊和肯尼亚鲁班工坊场地建设面积位居前三。柬埔寨鲁班工坊因为承载了面向澜湄五国的区域职业教育与培训，拥有18间实训教室，因此办学场地面积最大且为独栋楼设计。

三、教学保障不断加强

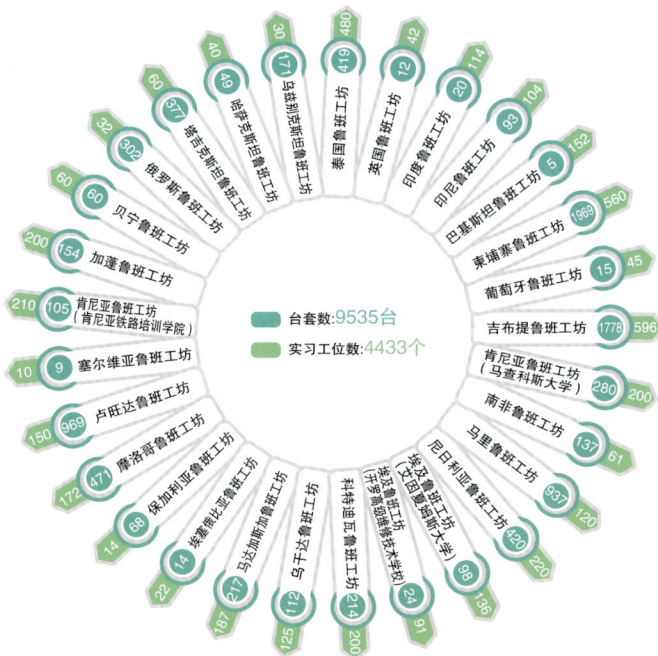

图4　鲁班工坊教学实训设备情况

先进的教学实训设备是鲁班工坊质量的重要保障，29个项目累计教学设备的总台套数达到9535台，其中新增台套1134台；为学生提供的实习工位总数达到4433个，其中新增工位993个。

通过这些增长可以看到，鲁班工坊在中外参建者的共同努力下，正在高速地发展。一是中外参建者持续性地投入资源，不断增加教学装备数量、更新升级技术，以适应新技术的发展和产业的需求；二是实习工位数的增长表明项目越来越重视对学生实践能力的培养，产教融合、校企合作理念在合作国被重视；三是新项目新专业的开设显示鲁班工坊面对市场需求变化不断拓展与适应。

四、课程资源开发持续推进

首先，课程开发。课程建设是鲁班工坊最核心的环节。至 2023 年底，全球 29 个鲁班工坊课程开发总量达到 534 门，这些课程均以先进的教学模式为依据，结合本土化需求而开发，不仅用于合作专业的学历教育，同时也用于其他专业选修以及社会和企业培训，因此适用广泛，对提升学生的就业竞争力、推进中外职业教育合作都具有重要的意义。

图 5　鲁班工坊国际课程资源开发情况

每个项目开发课程的规模受到其合作国产业发展水平，合作院校受益学生、教师、学员的需求，以及学历教育与职业培训制度要求等因素影响，每个项目课程开发的数量差异较大。泰国鲁班工坊、柬埔寨鲁班工坊、吉布提鲁班工坊、卢旺达鲁班工坊和巴基斯坦鲁班工坊的课程开发数量位居前五；在课程所属专业类别上，则是以铁路运维类课程和先进制造类课程开发规模最大，这也与合作国的产业需求紧密对接。

其次，教材开发。教材资源的建设直接关系鲁班工坊的教学质量和学生的学习效果。2023 年底，鲁班工坊公开出版的中外文双语教材达到 145 册，相关校本教材（含中外文自编实训讲义、工作手册等）达到 420 册。调查显示，活页式校本教材在所有鲁班工坊教育教学应用中最为普及，因其灵活的编写形式、模块化的内容设计，便于根据学生的实际情况和需求进行量身定制，使得鲁班工坊的教育教学更加贴合学生的学习背景和未来的职业发展。

最后，信息化资源开发。随着信息技术的飞速发展，教育领域正经历着一场深刻的变革。信息化教学资源建设对国际合作教育具有重大的意义，打破了时间和空间限制，充分满足海外学生、教师、社会与企业学员的专业学习需求。统计数据显示，目前鲁班工坊的信息化教学资源包括 PPT（总计 6518 个）、视频资源（总计 54641.7 分钟）和题库（总计 967 个）等。29 个项目中，信息化资源开发最多的前五位分别是埃及鲁班工坊、马达加斯加鲁班工坊、肯尼亚鲁班工坊、泰国鲁班工坊和马里鲁班工坊，信息化教学资源为鲁班工坊适应合作国不同学习者的不同学习需求提供了有力保障，同时也使得鲁班工坊的服务范围和服务形式有了更大的空间。

五、海外师资培训形成制度

海外师资培训是鲁班工坊建设的首要环节。多样化的培训不仅满足了专业教师不断提升教育技术、教学方法的需求，同时也为鲁班工坊教育质量的提升奠定了坚实的基础。统计数据显示，2016—2023 年，外方专业教师来华培训和本土培训的规模达到 3308 人次，为其开设的专业培训与企业实践课程总时长达到 248073.2 小时，其中参加在线培训的海外专业教师为 1654 人次。

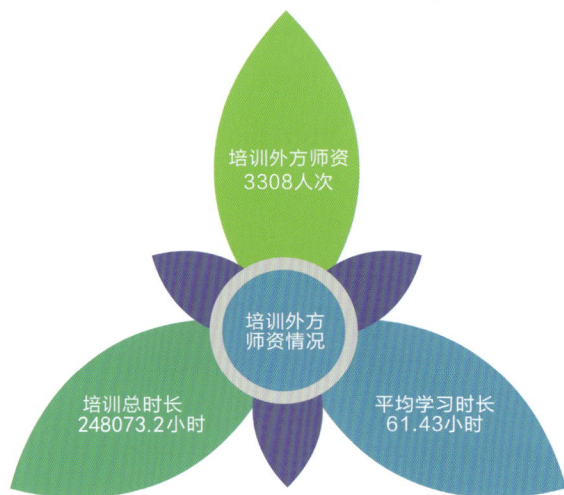

图 6　合作国专业教师培训情况

研推中心经过实地访谈调查发现，海外专业教师对培训给予了很高的投入，表示持续性的培训助其更新了教学理念，掌握了新的教学方法，拓宽了国际视野，同时与中方专业教师互学互鉴，促进了中外双方院校的专业教育改革，增强了跨文化交流能力。这些能力的提升，直接促进了教学质量的提高，使得学生们能够接受到更加优质的教育。

六、双语师资规模不断提升

鲁班工坊不仅将中国优秀的教育资源、教育技术与国际分享，在中外交流的过程中，中国专业教师的教学能力尤其是双语教学的能力也实现了飞跃式的提高。据研推中心的统计显示，目前鲁班工坊项目中双语教师的人数高达 559 人，其中泰国鲁班工坊、肯尼亚鲁班工坊、卢旺达鲁班工坊的双语教师数量排名前三。

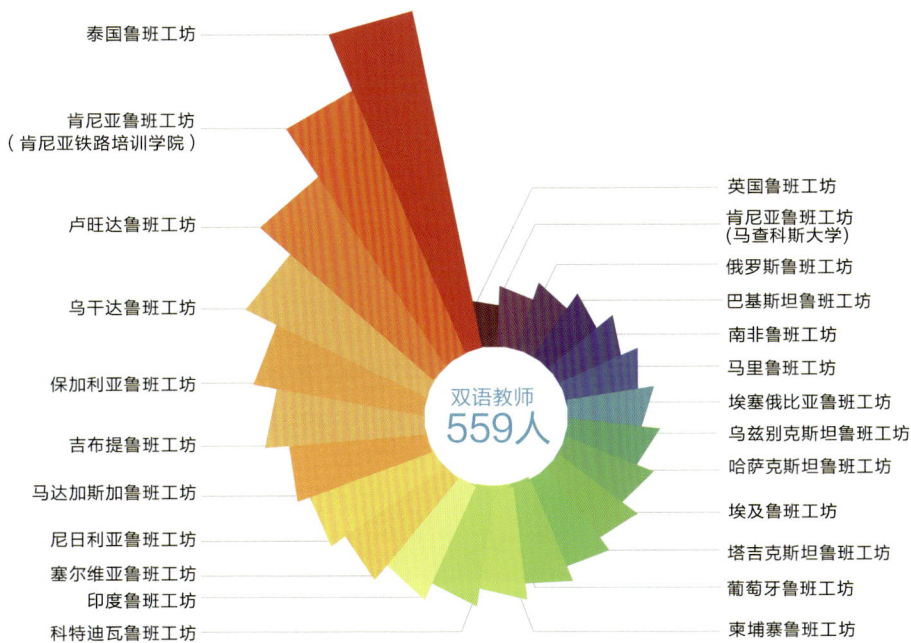

图 7　双语专业教师情况

泰国鲁班工坊
肯尼亚鲁班工坊
（肯尼亚铁路培训学院）
卢旺达鲁班工坊
乌干达鲁班工坊
保加利亚鲁班工坊
吉布提鲁班工坊
马达加斯加鲁班工坊
尼日利亚鲁班工坊
塞尔维亚鲁班工坊
印度鲁班工坊
科特迪瓦鲁班工坊

英国鲁班工坊
肯尼亚鲁班工坊
（马查科斯大学）
俄罗斯鲁班工坊
巴基斯坦鲁班工坊
南非鲁班工坊
马里鲁班工坊
埃塞俄比亚鲁班工坊
乌兹别克斯坦鲁班工坊
哈萨克斯坦鲁班工坊
埃及鲁班工坊
塔吉克斯坦鲁班工坊
葡萄牙鲁班工坊
柬埔寨鲁班工坊

双语教师
559人

　　实践表明，双语教师采用熟练的双语进行专业授课，更有利于帮助学生理解不同国别背景下的技术学习思维方式，培养学生具备全球视野。同时，双语教师还承担着协调中外专业教育、促进中外人文交流的责任，通过与来自不同国家和地区的教育管理者和专业教学教师进行有效沟通，助力中外院校对鲁班工坊的日常教学进行组织管理，共同制订长远发展规划。

第三章
人才培养与教育教学质量

一、学历教育与培训规模化发展

鲁班工坊合作办学包括学历教育和非学历教育。学历教育方面，截至 2023 年 12 月，鲁班工坊已累计为 17558 名合作专业学生和选修课程学生提供了学历教育，其中包括来华留学生 570 人和本土学生 16988 人。

受到合作国教育政策和产业发展需求等因素影响，各国学历生的规模有较大不同，一些国家如塔吉克斯坦、印度、柬埔寨、埃及、科特迪瓦、乌干达和埃塞俄比亚等亚洲和非洲国家的学历教育学生数量相对较多。截至 2023 年 12 月，鲁班工坊总在校生规模为 11371 人，中外专业教师合作为学生开发了系统的课程，学生在工坊学习了系统的课程，在工坊能够接受完整的知识、技术教育，包括专业基础理论课和综合实践课。

开展的多样化职业培训是鲁班工坊助力各国提升人力资源素质、促进经济发展的重要路径。研推中心的统计数据显示，鲁班工坊已累计培训 95421 人次，其中定制化为企业员工进行的培训规模达到 7429 人次，面向社会、师生等培训规模达到 87992 人次，充分展示了鲁班工坊积极履行社会责任，通过提供企业培训和社会培训帮助当地员工提升技能，助力本土社会经济发展。

图 8　鲁班工坊人才培养情况　　　　　图 9　鲁班工坊培训情况

在培训方式上，非学历教育所提供的职业培训、短期课程、工作坊等为在职人员提供了提升自我、更新知识的平台。在技术手段上，采取线上线下相互结合的方式，充分应用信息技术为更多的企业员工和社会人员提供有针对性的培训服务，以其灵活多变的形式，满足了合作国对多样化技术技能培训的需求。统计数据显示，非学历教育培训的规模在不同国家和地区之间存在显著差异，泰国、印度、吉布提等国家的职业培训人次和规模相对较大，特别是泰国，其培训人次远超其他国家，其影响力已经超出区域与国家范围，在东盟形成一定影响力。几年的实践显示，信息技术的应用能够极大地拓展培训的范围，但也存在一定的质量问题，不能确保教学质量与传统的线下培训有同等效果，这也是未来培训需要解决的问题之一。

二、人才培养质量持续稳步提升[①]

鲁班工坊的建设不仅关注学生的就业，也支持学生的个人发展和职业规划。自 2018 年首届鲁班工坊学生毕业以来，截至 2023 年全球鲁班工坊已有

---

① 国家社会科学基金青年项目"'双循环'新格局下基于'鲁班工坊'推进中国引领全球职业教育治理体系建设研究"（21CGL042）的研究成果。

6000 余名学历生毕业，毕业生一部分在合作国当地企业就业，一部分继续升学。受外部环境和信息来源影响，天津市鲁班工坊不完全统计显示，本土就业的毕业生规模为 3263 名。这些毕业生由于接受了高质量的学历教育与职业培训，掌握先进的行业技术技能，能够熟练应用技术装备并具备一定研发能力，成为本地区具有较强就业竞争力的青年，这一成果在区域经济增长较快的印度尼西亚和巴基斯坦等国较为显著。调查显示，另一部分毕业生则通过国家考试进入高一级院校继续深造，升学形式多样，既包括从中职升入高职，也包括高职升入应用本科，以及本科升入研究生，升学较多的为泰国鲁班工坊、印度尼西亚鲁班工坊、柬埔寨鲁班工坊和葡萄牙鲁班工坊等。

师生满意度调查。高素质技术技能人才培养是全球鲁班工坊建设的核心内涵。总体而言，鲁班工坊经过 7 年的高质量建设与稳步发展，人才培养成效明显。第一，师生对鲁班工坊人才培养全过程给予高度肯定。鲁班工坊师生均认为，鲁班工坊人才培养目标能够满足多元需求，满足学生发展需求的比例最高，分别为 88.14% 和 86.24%，有 88.18% 的鲁班工坊学生对教学方式满意；在人才培养效果方面，鲁班工坊学生认为多元因素能够影响自身未来职业发展，其中专业设置满足企业需要（73.26%）、课程内容丰富实用性强（67.25%）、教师能力较强且学习效果理想（62.98%）是鲁班工坊学生认为能够影响自身未来职业发展的最重要的三个因素。鲁班工坊学生在就业（36.24%）和升学（45.74%）意愿中均表现出了对中国的向往，83.92% 的学生认为鲁班工坊在当地很受欢迎，鲁班工坊已经成为非常重要的民生项目。第二，毕业生对学业成就获得满意度给予很高评价。通过鲁班工坊人才培养，鲁班工坊毕业生在信息获取和运用能力、人际交往能力、技术应用能力、资源管理能力、统筹能力等五个关键能力的获得感较强，比例分别达到 76.54%、72.63%、65.92%、56.42% 和 28.49%。第三，毕业生对就业满意度给予积极评价。总体而言，有 87.15% 的鲁班工坊毕业生对工作满意，高达 91.62% 的鲁班工坊毕业生完全能够适应单位的工作环境，高达 92.74% 的鲁班工坊毕业生认为鲁班工坊的学习经历有益于扩展未来工作发展空间。调查最终显示，高达 91.62% 的鲁班工坊毕业生对鲁班工坊的推荐度很高。

（一）鲁班工坊师生对鲁班工坊人才培养全过程给予高度肯定

鲁班工坊教学一线教师和鲁班工坊学生在人才培养专业设置与目标设置、教学组织与实施、人才培养效果方面均给予充分肯定。

第一，在人才培养专业设置与目标设置方面，教学一线教师、学生均认为鲁班工坊人才培养目标能够满足多元需求，其中，鲁班工坊师生均认为鲁班工坊人才培养目标能够满足学生发展需求的比例最高，分别为 88.14% 和 86.24%（图 10、图 11）。数据表明，鲁班工坊的建设与发展以学生为中心，教学一线教师和学生均将学生发展需求置于首要位置。对比发现，鲁班工坊师生对于人才培养目标的评价较为一致。

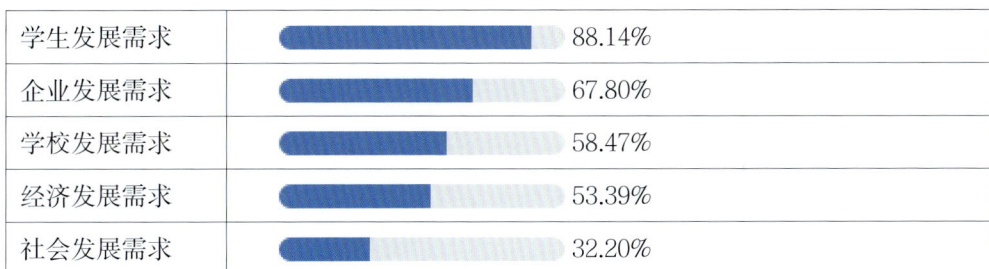

学生发展需求	88.14%
企业发展需求	67.80%
学校发展需求	58.47%
经济发展需求	53.39%
社会发展需求	32.20%

图 10　教师对于人才培养目标能够满足多元需求的评价情况

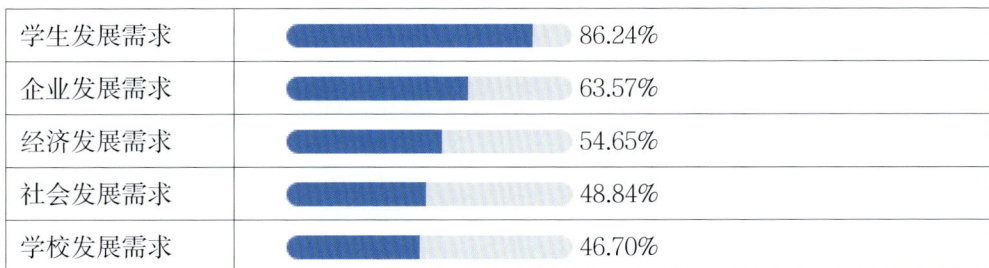

学生发展需求	86.24%
企业发展需求	63.57%
经济发展需求	54.65%
社会发展需求	48.84%
学校发展需求	46.70%

图 11　学生对于人才培养目标能够满足多元需求的评价情况

第二，在教学组织与实施方面，在教学内容上，课程是最核心的教学内容。在学生调查中，鲁班工坊学生对于鲁班工坊的课程设置满意度较高，其中，课程实用性强（79.26%）、课程内容设置合理（51.94%）、课程时间设计合理（50.19%）、理论课和实践课的比例协调（50.00%）是鲁班工坊学生对于鲁班工坊的课程设置最满意的 4 个方面（图 12）。数据表明，鲁班工坊的建设目标是为合作国家培养高素质劳动者和技术技能人才，所以在课程设置中高度重视课程实用性建设，并且该因素也成为鲁班工坊学生对课程建设最满意的方面。

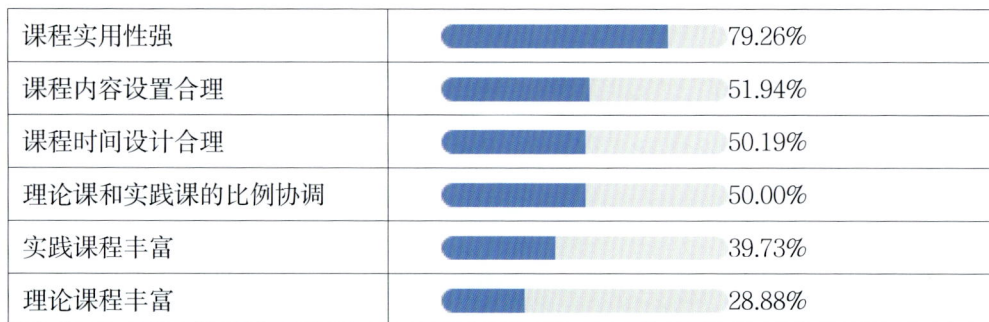

课程实用性强		79.26%
课程内容设置合理		51.94%
课程时间设计合理		50.19%
理论课和实践课的比例协调		50.00%
实践课程丰富		39.73%
理论课程丰富		28.88%

图 12　学生对于课程设置的评价情况

在教学方式上，79.67% 的教学一线教师认为自己能够熟练地将 EPIP 教学方式应用到教学中（图 13）；88.18% 的鲁班工坊学生对鲁班工坊教学方式满意（图 14）。

在教学资源上，教学装备（85.85%）、双语教材（77.91%）、在线课

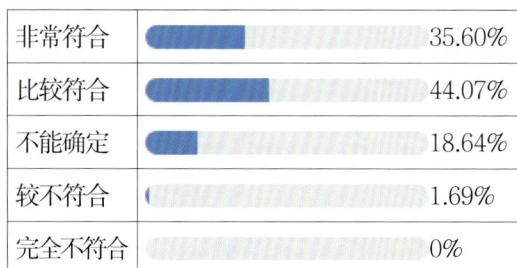

非常符合	35.60%
比较符合	44.07%
不能确定	18.64%
较不符合	1.69%
完全不符合	0%

图 13　教师对于熟练应用 EPIP 教学方式
的评价情况

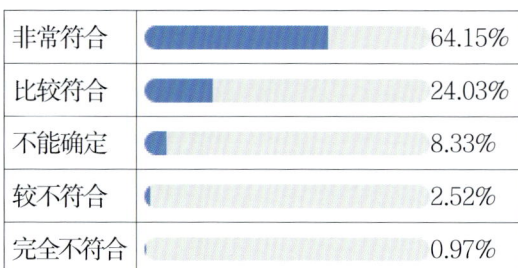

非常符合	64.15%
比较符合	24.03%
不能确定	8.33%
较不符合	2.52%
完全不符合	0.97%

图 14　学生对于教学方式十分满意的评价情况

程（74.22%）是鲁班工坊学生对鲁班工坊教学资源最满意的 3 个方面（图 15）。数据表明，相对于鲁班工坊教学资源建设中的"软"资源而言，教学装备等"硬"资源建设更能获得鲁班工坊学生的满意。

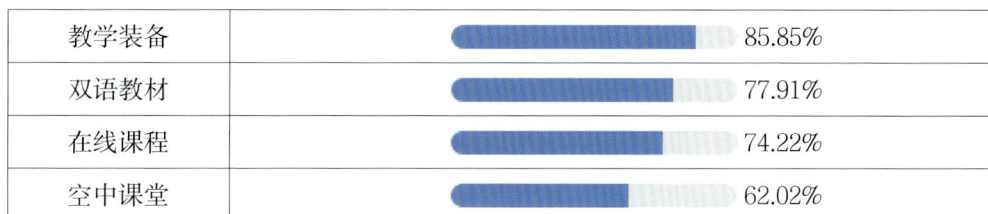

教学装备		85.85%
双语教材		77.91%
在线课程		74.22%
空中课堂		62.02%

图 15　学生对于教学资源的评价情况

鲁班工坊学生对于鲁班工坊授课教师的教学水平给予了积极评价，其中，教学态度端正（73.45%）、教学效果良好（58.33%）、教学方法多样（55.23%）是鲁班工坊学生认为教师教学水平最令自己满意的 3 个方面（图 16）。数据表明，在鲁班工坊教学水平的评价中，教学一线教师给予学生非常充分的人文关怀，所以教学态度端正成为鲁班工坊学生最满意的方面。

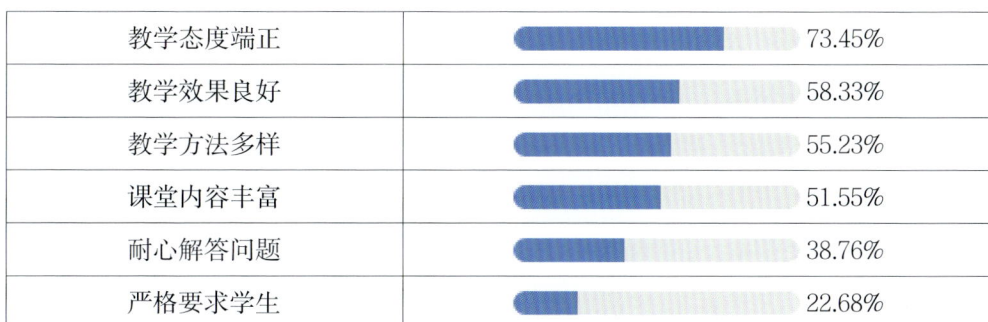

教学态度端正		73.45%
教学效果良好		58.33%
教学方法多样		55.23%
课堂内容丰富		51.55%
耐心解答问题		38.76%
严格要求学生		22.68%

图 16　学生对于教师教学水平的评价情况

在教学培训上，在被调查的鲁班工坊教学一线教师中，全部教师接受了鲁班工坊教学的教师培训，只是培训地点和培训教师不同。其中，在中国接受培训的教师占 26.27%，在本国接受培训且培训教师为中国教师的占

27.97%，在本国接受培训且培训教师为本国教师的占 45.76%（图 17）。数据表明，大部分鲁班工坊教学一线教师是在本国接受教学培训，未来需要进一步提升教学一线教师来中国接受教学培训的比例，进而提升教学质量。

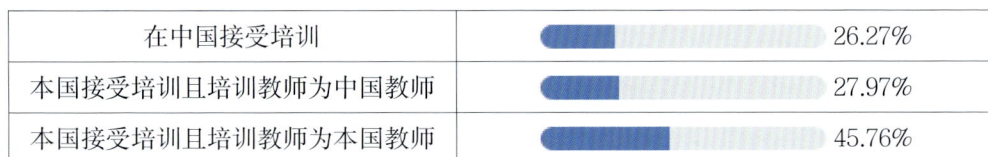

在中国接受培训		26.27%
本国接受培训且培训教师为中国教师		27.97%
本国接受培训且培训教师为本国教师		45.76%

图 17　教师的教师培训情况

第三，在人才培养效果方面，在教学效果上，教学一线教师认为先进的教学设备（86.44%）、合适的教学材料（65.25%）、清晰的教学目标（60.17%）是影响鲁班工坊教学效果的 3 个主要因素（图 18）。数据表明，作为"五到位"的重要内容之一，"设备到位"对于教学效果具有重要影响。

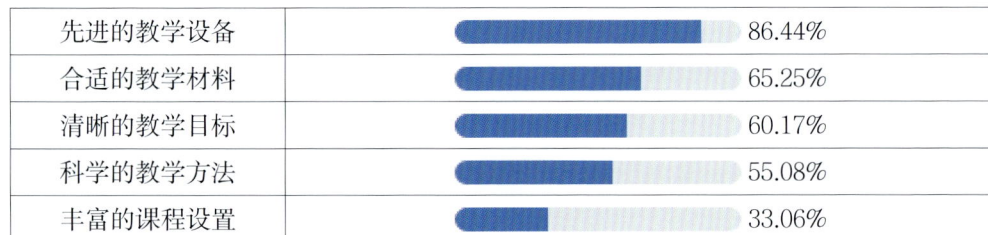

先进的教学设备		86.44%
合适的教学材料		65.25%
清晰的教学目标		60.17%
科学的教学方法		55.08%
丰富的课程设置		33.06%

图 18　教师对于影响教学效果因素的评价情况

鲁班工坊学生毕业后的主要流向包括就业和升学两种趋势。职业教育的重要目标之一就是帮助学生实现高质量就业。在学生调查中，鲁班工坊学生认为多元因素能够影响自身未来职业发展，其中，专业设置满足企业需要（73.26%）、课程内容丰富且实用性强（67.25%）、教师能力较强且学习效果理想（62.98%）是鲁班工坊学生认为能够影响自身未来职业发展的最重要的 3 个因素（图 19）。数据表明，鲁班工坊建设深度服务国际产能合作，基于产教融合的校企合作为合作国家供给技术技能人才支持，促进合作国家产业转型升级，所以专业设置满足企业需要成为影响鲁班工坊学生职业发展的最重要的因素。

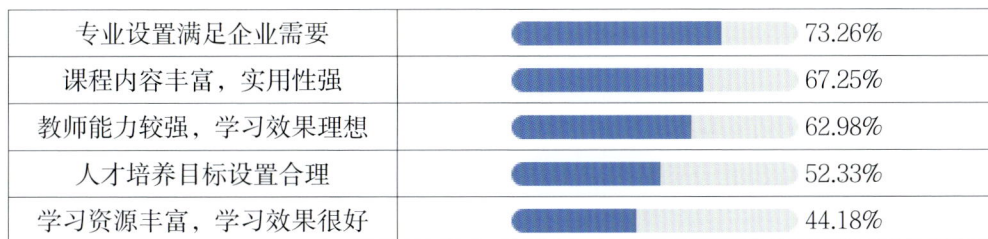

专业设置满足企业需要		73.26%
课程内容丰富，实用性强		67.25%
教师能力较强，学习效果理想		62.98%
人才培养目标设置合理		52.33%
学习资源丰富，学习效果很好		44.18%

图 19　学生对于影响职业发展因素的评价情况

鲁班工坊学生对于未来的就业预期，36.24% 的鲁班工坊学生想去中资企业就业，22.48% 的鲁班工坊学生想去本国企业就业，20.54% 的鲁班工坊学生想去合资企业就业（图 20）。数据表明，想去中资企业就业成为鲁班工坊学生最重要的就业预期。

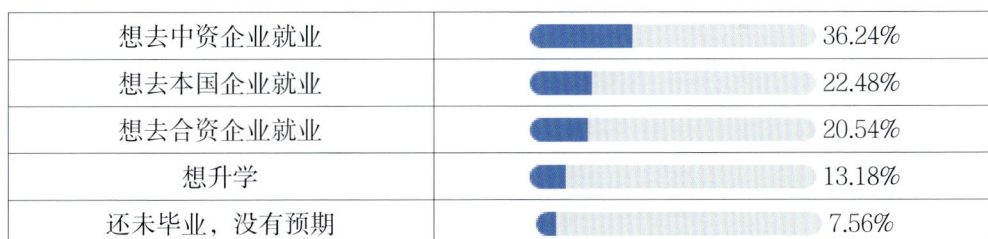

想去中资企业就业		36.24%
想去本国企业就业		22.48%
想去合资企业就业		20.54%
想升学		13.18%
还未毕业，没有预期		7.56%

图 20　学生对于未来就业的预期情况

鲁班工坊学生的升学意愿也表现出了对中国的向往。调查显示，45.74% 的鲁班工坊学生想去中国继续上学，32.75% 的鲁班工坊学生想在本国继续上学，15.89% 的鲁班工坊学生想去非中国、非本国的其他国家继续上学，5.62% 的鲁班工坊学生没有升学意愿（图 21）。数据表明，想去中国继续上学成为鲁班工坊学生最重要的升学预期。

想去中国继续上学		45.74%
想在本国继续上学		32.75%
想去非中国、非本国的其他国家继续上学		15.89%
没有升学意愿		5.62%

图 21 学生对于升学的意愿情况

鲁班工坊学生对于鲁班工坊在当地很受欢迎的评价中，58.53% 的鲁班工坊学生认为非常符合，25.39% 的鲁班工坊学生认为比较符合，两者之和占到全部被调查学生总数的 83.92%（图 22）。数据表明，鲁班工坊在当地很受欢迎，是非常重要的民生项目。

非常符合		58.53%
比较符合		25.39%
不能确定		13.37%
较不符合		1.74%
完全不符合		0.97%

图 22 学生对于鲁班工坊很受欢迎的评价情况

（二）鲁班工坊毕业生的人才培养满意度和学业成就获得满意度实现双高评价

第一，鲁班工坊毕业生对人才培养满意度评价很高。鲁班工坊毕业生认为实习实训实用性强的比例为 74.30%，认为课程内容设置合理的比例为 70.95%，认为教师教学能力很强的比例为 69.27%，认为教学方法丰富多样的比例为 50.28%，认为教学资源非常丰富的比例为 35.20%（图 23）。数据显示，实习实训实用性强是鲁班工坊毕业生对于鲁班工坊人才培养最满意的方面，这也与鲁班工坊学生对课程建设最满意的方面是课程实用性强的评价相一致。

实习实训实用性强		74.30%
课程内容设置合理		70.95%
教师教学能力很强		69.27%
教学方法丰富多样		50.28%
教学资源非常丰富		35.20%

图 23 毕业生对于人才培养的评价情况

第二，鲁班工坊毕业生对学业成就获得满意度评价很高。总体而言，通过鲁班工坊人才培养，鲁班工坊毕业生在信息获取和运用能力、人际交往能力、技术应用能力、资源管理能力、统筹能力等 5 个方面的关键能力上的获得感较强，比例分别达到 76.54%、72.63%、65.92%、56.42% 和 28.49%（图 24）。数据表明，在数字时代，鲁班工坊毕业生的信息获取和运用能力的获得感最强。

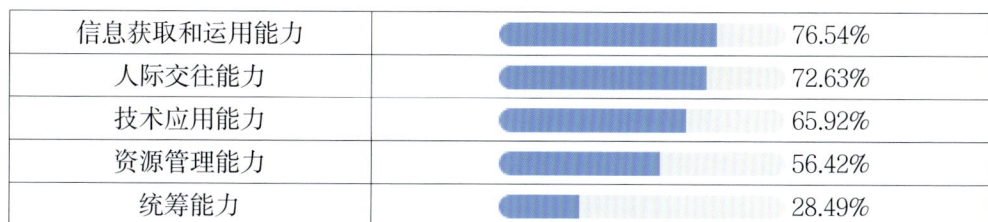

信息获取和运用能力	76.54%
人际交往能力	72.63%
技术应用能力	65.92%
资源管理能力	56.42%
统筹能力	28.49%

图 24　毕业生对于自己能力提升的评价情况

（三）鲁班工坊毕业生对就业满意度给予积极评价

鲁班工坊毕业生的就业满意度较高。总体而言，有 87.15% 的鲁班工坊毕业生对工作满意（图 25）。

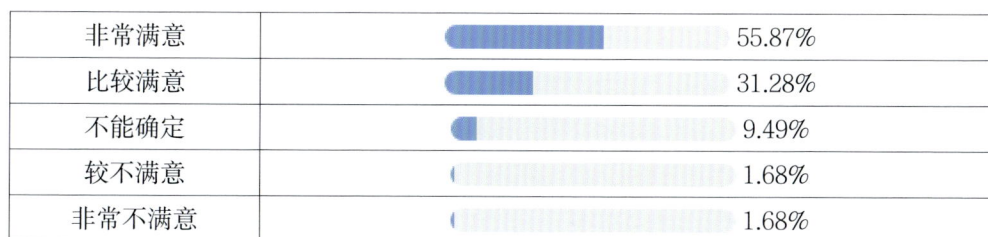

非常满意	55.87%
比较满意	31.28%
不能确定	9.49%
较不满意	1.68%
非常不满意	1.68%

图 25　毕业生对于工作总体满意度的评价情况

在工作环境适应性方面，高达 91.62% 的鲁班工坊毕业生完全能够适应单位的工作环境（图 26）；在未来工作发展空间方面，高达 92.74% 的鲁班工坊毕业生认为鲁班工坊的学习经历有益于扩展未来工作发展空间（图 27）。

完全能够		73.74%
比较能够		17.88%
不能确定		6.15%
比较不能够		0%
完全不能够		2.23%

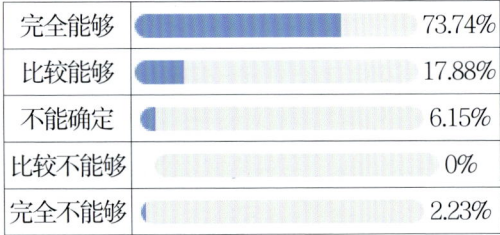

图 26　毕业生对于自己是否能适应单位工作
环境的评价情况

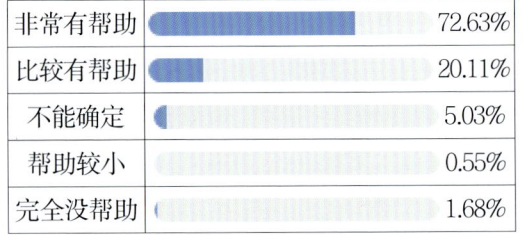

非常有帮助		72.63%
比较有帮助		20.11%
不能确定		5.03%
帮助较小		0.55%
完全没帮助		1.68%

图 27　毕业生对于学习经历是否有益于
工作发展的评价情况

调查最终显示，高达 91.62% 的鲁班工坊毕业生对鲁班工坊的推荐度很高（图 28）。数据表明，鲁班工坊已经成为民生项目，获得了当地学生的高度好评。

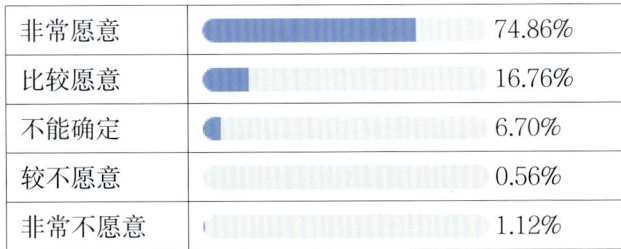

非常愿意		74.86%
比较愿意		16.76%
不能确定		6.70%
较不愿意		0.56%
非常不愿意		1.12%

图 28　毕业生对于是否愿意将鲁班工坊推荐给亲朋好友去就读的评价情况

第四章
深化交流合作提升影响力

一、中外师生共同参加技能竞赛

凭借优质的教育教学，鲁班工坊中外合作院校的师生在国内外各类技能竞赛中取得了优异的成绩，获奖数量逐年递增，尤其是金牌数量日益增多。中外师生在各级各类比赛中获奖总数达到 1550 人次，其中，中外教师获奖 1014 人次，中外学生获奖 536 人次。

技能大赛涉及广泛。国际性大赛主要包括首届世界职业院校技能大赛、"一带一路"暨金砖国家技能发展与技术创新大赛、中国国际"互联网+"大学生创新创业大赛、东盟技能大赛等，国家层面的技术技能大赛包括全国职业院校技能大赛、俄罗斯－"复杂系统中的信息技术"互联网奥林匹克竞赛、塔吉克斯坦"科学－知识之光"竞赛、泰国职业技能大赛、印度尼西亚国家级自动化生产线大赛、启诚杯第四届中国 EPIP Micromouse 国际邀请赛暨电脑国际大赛中国地区选拔赛等。在这些面向全球或者区域的技术技能竞赛上，鲁班工坊参建院校的师生成绩突出，金奖获奖数量不断攀升。这些荣誉和成就不仅彰显了鲁班工坊在培养国际化技能型人才方面的显著成效，也为未来中外合作办学提供了良好的基础。

A

1.世界职业院校技能大赛
2.世界机器人大赛锦标赛
3.金砖国家职业技能大赛
4."一带一路"暨金砖国家技能发展与技术创新大赛
5.全国职业院校教师技能大赛
6.全国行业职业技能竞赛
7.全国数字创意教学技能大赛
8.全国人工智能应用技术技能大赛
9.全国职业技能大赛
10.全国职业院校技能大赛国际邀请赛
11.启诚杯EPIP鲁班工坊国际邀请赛
12.机械行业职业教育技能大赛国际组比赛
13.工程实践创新项目师生挑战赛

B

1.世界职业院校技能大赛
2."一带一路"暨金砖国家技能发展与技术创新大赛
3.国际智能体育大会
4.中非（埃塞）大学生工业机器人技术应用友谊赛
5.泰国职业技能和基础技能大赛
6.泰国首届铁道运输系统邀请赛
7.吉布提鲁班工坊职业技能大赛
8.启诚杯EPIP鲁班工坊国际邀请赛
9.启诚杯电脑鼠国际邀请赛
10.俄罗斯－"复杂系统中的信息技术"互联网奥林匹克竞赛
11.俄罗斯计算机安全竞赛
12.俄罗斯第六届全国大学生校际锦标赛
13.塔吉克斯坦"科学–知识之光"竞赛
14.印尼技能大赛

图 29　鲁班工坊师生技能竞赛情况

二、中外参建院校荣获政府奖项

　　鲁班工坊的国际影响力是巨大的，得到了中外政府的高度认可。一方面，为表彰项目为当地经济社会发展所作出的巨大贡献，合作国政府给予鲁班工坊参建中方院校各种荣誉，典型的如泰国鲁班工坊中方院校天津渤海职业技术学院和天津铁道职业技术学院获得泰国诗琳通公主纪念奖章、泰国职业教育委员会杰出贡献奖和泰国大城省政府杰出贡献奖；柬埔寨鲁班工坊中方参建院校中德应用技术大学获得柬埔寨王国政府萨哈梅特里军官和骑士勋章，柬埔寨劳工部突出贡献奖；塞尔维亚鲁班工坊中方参建院校浙江旅游职业学院获得世界职业院校与技术大学联盟（WFCP）卓越奖，等等。另一方面，中国政府也给予作出突出贡献的外方院校高度肯定，泰国大城技术学院原院长因其在首个鲁班工坊的创立与发展，推动中泰人文交流与国际产教融合作出的巨大贡献，于 2023 年获得中国政府友谊奖。

三、举办丰富多样人文交流活动

促进中外人文交流是鲁班工坊的重任之一。师生互访、中外联合组队参赛、举办学术论坛等是鲁班工坊人文交流的主要形式，通过形式多样的交流方式打破了地域的限制，为来自不同国家的师生、官员、学者和企业家等搭建交流平台。截至 2023 年底，中外师生交流总量 8216 人次，线下师生交流中学生互访 741 人次、教师互访 1589 人次，其余为线上交流。参加各级各类技术技能竞赛交流的中外师生总量为 1200 人次，其中参赛中外专业教师 131 人次，学生 1069 人次。

2023 年在葡萄牙举办"一带一路"职业教育国际合作与发展论坛，来自葡萄牙高等教育、塞图巴尔市政府官员，以及葡萄牙鲁班工坊中外参建院校代表、葡语系合作大学代表和天津市教育科学研究院专家，以"创新、融合、发展"为主题，共同探讨如何以国际项目为载体，推动中葡国际合作与交流。中外专家提出，应在两个方面加强合作：一是加强在专业应用技术领域的科研与教育合作，促进中外师生交流，为学生营造多元化国际教育环境，形成超越国界的相互理解，实现共同进步；二是成立葡萄牙鲁班工坊校企联盟，借助先进的技术设备强化与国际企业紧密合作，有针对性地为企业提出解决方案，实现共赢。

四、项目受到中外媒体广泛关注

鲁班工坊的建设从开始创立就得到各国政府和社会组织的高度关注，中外媒体给予了持续性的报道。据研推中心不完全统计，目前累计在国内外权威媒体的报道次数达到 2067 次。

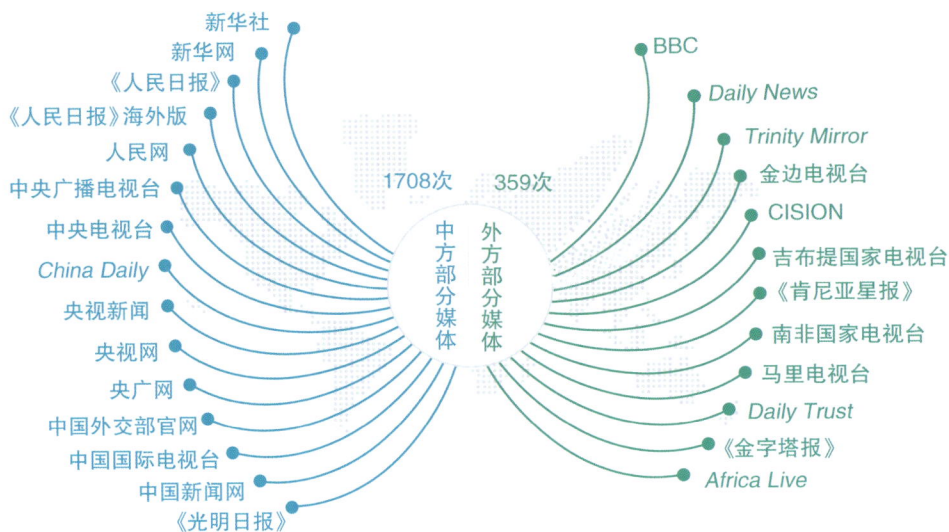

图 30　全球媒体宣传报道情况

泰国的 Siam Rath online news、Daily News，印度尼西亚的《暹罗日报》，英国的 BBC，印度的 Trinity Mirror，柬埔寨的《和平岛日报》、金边电视台，葡萄牙的 CISION、Conta Loios、Wintech、PCGUIA、SAPO 门户网站，吉布提国家电视台、《吉布提国家报》、南非国家电视台等传统媒体和新媒体都对鲁班工坊的建设与发展进行了持续性报道。如今，越来越多的合作国家重视鲁班工坊的建设与发展，将其作为中外民心相通的友谊之桥。

第五章
深化产教融合助力区域发展

一、服务企业内涵式高质量发展

实施国际产教融合是鲁班工坊助力国际产能合作的核心内容，也是鲁班工坊建设与发展的基本原则。随着劳动力市场国际化程度的不断提高，技术技能人才在全球范围内流动成为不可避免的趋势，迫切需要强化产教融合、校企合作，促进各国技术的共同提升。实施产教融合既是促进本土经济、国际产能合作的重要路径，也是世界各国职业教育实现高质量发展的一种有效方式。

当前，我国已与80多个国家签署了"一带一路"合作协议，同30多个国家开展了机制化产能合作，在24个共建国家推进建设75个境外经贸合作区，创造了近20万个就业岗位，对全球发展正在产生积极和深远影响。无论是"一带一路"国际产能合作还是鲁班工坊在地国的产业发展，都需要加快职业教育发展，培养高素质本土化人才，为全球经济实现持续发展提供人才支撑。

截至2023年底，鲁班工坊已累计面向各类企业和社会的培训总量为9.54万人次，培训类型多样化，包括定制式专项培训、社会培训等，培训方式既有线下培训也包括网络培训，目前累计的线上培训规模达到13699人次，服务范围不断扩大。

29个鲁班工坊每年为区域培养急需的学历教育学生规模达万人以上，涵盖中职、高职、应用本科和研究生四个层次，有效地满足了当地企业对紧缺专业技术技能人才的迫切需求，以及所在地域的院校师生、社会人员对职业技能培训的要求。

国际产教融合校企合作的根本目的是服务合作国和区域的经济社会发展，鲁班工坊的建设紧紧围绕两国或者多国区域经济社会发展规划和产业升级需求，通过人才培养、技术创新等多种形式，来助力其发展。调查显示，基于鲁班工坊的国际校企合作是深度融合的，合作企业深度参与鲁班工坊的建设与发展，将企业的技术标准、工艺技术等融入从专业标准的设计到课程资源的开发，以及教学的组织与实施的教育教学全过程，使得鲁班工坊的教育教学完全契合国际经济社会发展的实际需求，为其培养了具有竞争力的本土化技术技能人才。

二、服务产业发展典型案例分析

典型一

鲁班工坊为区域协同发展提供动力。典型的如为澜湄合作而创建的柬埔寨鲁班工坊，其建设定位于立足柬埔寨、服务澜湄五国、辐射东盟十国，集职业教育、职业培训、科学研究、文化传承、创新创业五位一体，按照市场化运作的国际化职业教育中心。

典型二

鲁班工坊服务非洲铁路与轨道交通产业的发展。以天津铁道职业技术学院为例，自2019年吉布提鲁班工坊和尼日利亚鲁班工坊创建以来，为亚吉铁路当地员工开设线路工、信号工、通信工等8个工种的线上教育培训，2967位本土员工取得培训结业证书；2022—2023年，完成亚吉铁路那噶德车站铁路员工、亚吉铁路高层管理人员培训，为亚吉铁路在"一带一路"十周年之际实现非洲本土化运营提供了有力保障。

典型三

　　服务南亚农业技术的发展。典型的如巴基斯坦鲁班工坊，项目定位于服务巴基斯坦"超级大省"旁遮普省工业现代技术人才培养和农业机械化转型升级。国际企业勇猛机械公司与项目参建单位协同合作，紧紧围绕巴基斯坦农业发展的现状，开发了适用课程标准，研发了设计的农机装备，助力当地农业机械化应用推广与技术创新，凭借强动力、高性能和智能化的农机产品，其技术在巴基斯坦被广泛认可。

第六章
国际品牌打造与发展策略

从 2018 年 9 月 3 日中非合作论坛北京峰会宣布要在非洲设立 10 个鲁班工坊，向非洲青年提供职业技能培训，到 2023 年 10 月 18 日第三届"一带一路"国际合作高峰论坛开幕式宣布高质量共建"一带一路"八项行动，一系列重大外交场合均提出了通过鲁班工坊等推进中外职业教育合作。鲁班工坊作为职业教育在中外人文交流领域的标志性成果，正在发挥更大的作用，推动着中外友谊的不断加深。

一、加强全球知识产权保护

持续推进知识产权保护工作。强化法律保护，积极维护品牌声誉是鲁班工坊品牌发展的重要保障，鲁班工坊要进一步强化法律保护，致力于通过多层次、多维度的策略来强化品牌管理，确保其品牌形象的统一性和权威性，不断提高品牌的声誉。目前，在英国成功注册了第一个国际鲁班工坊商标，这对保护鲁班工坊品牌在国际社会的权益具有重要意义。我国已经在海外创立了 29 个项目，涉及亚洲、欧洲和非洲国家，不同国家品牌保护申请要求不同，因此要全面保护其合法权益迫切需要加快进行中外商标权申请，使鲁班工坊在项目所在国获得全面的知识产权保护，从而维护全球鲁班工坊建设的市场秩序、保护参建各方的权益、促进项目持续发展，提升鲁班工坊的品牌形象和社会公信力。

二、完善内部运行管理机制

职业教育的国际合作面临诸多不确定因素，亟待建立健全项目运营管理体制机制，强化项目参建各方协同管理、共建共享鲁班工坊办学体制与运行机制，通过规范的多方合作协议、章程及教学文件、实验实训室管理制度等，将参建各方的权利义务、学历教育与对外培训等实际要求融入其中，使鲁班工坊项目运行更加科学规范，确保项目建设的发展定位、组织运行、资源投入等关键要素严格遵循鲁班工坊的内涵发展要求，推动项目在专业教育、校企合作、人文交流等方面高质量可持续推进，实现品牌内涵价值的统一性。

三、健全项目质量评估制度

在鲁班工坊建设规程中明确规定，鲁班工坊实行项目制管理，每三年为一个项目周期。2022年，在首届世界职业技术教育发展大会期间，在多国驻华使节的共同见证下，全球首批鲁班工坊运营认证授牌，22个鲁班工坊进入建设周期。如何对项目三年后的建设质量进行科学评估，以评促建、以评促改、评建结合，确保项目高质量发展是需要进行系统地科学研究与实践探索的。

天津市鲁班工坊研究与推广中心从2021年启动鲁班工坊试点评估科学研究与实验工作以来，结合项目所在国家的经济社会发展水平、合作院校的特点等因素，对8个项目进行试点探索。经过三年的实践，已经初步形成一套较为完整的、体系化的质量评估标准和机制。一方面，建议鲁班工坊建设联盟以天津经验为基础，广泛征求专家学者和项目参建各方的意见建议，修正完善评估指标体系、优化评估流程与机制，形成兼具科学性、客观性和公正性的鲁班工坊质量评估标准体系，在全球范围鲁班工坊中实施应用。另一方面，建立相应的管理制度体系，一是实施过程检查和结果评估，在专家组的帮助下，通过专家组对鲁班工坊建设过程和实际运行效果进行全面客观的评价分析,帮助项目组不断总结经验、及时发现问题,并明确下一步整改方向;二是严格管理制度,项目三年建设期满,符合质量保障条件的,可以续接下一个项目周期,未能达到要求的则在规定时限内按照要求进行整改。

四、持续强化实证科学研究

鲁班工坊的建设从创建伊始就是与科学研究同步发展的,一方面大量的探索性实践为项目的发展提供可借鉴的经验,另一方面系统地科学研究为项目发展提供智库服务和科学指引。天津市鲁班工坊研究与推广中心至今已连续三年研究出版年度《鲁班工坊建设与发展报告》和《鲁班工坊建设发展概览(中英双语版)》[《鲁班工坊发展蓝皮书(中英双语版)],采用问卷调查、师生访谈等多种研究方式,翔实分析记录鲁班工坊的发展现状与建设成就,为参建各方学习借鉴提供参考。

未来,应进一步加强海外项目的实证研究,通过对中外双方学校、教师、学生、合作企业、政府部门及社会组织的综合性调研,结合不同国别鲁班工坊的建设背景,梳理分析共同特征与个性特点,从鲁班工坊项目的建设模式、人才培养、校企合作和人文交流等多个方面进行深入分析,总结成功经验、发现存在问题、分析制约因素、提出改革策略,为鲁班工坊的可持续、高水平发展提供科学依据。

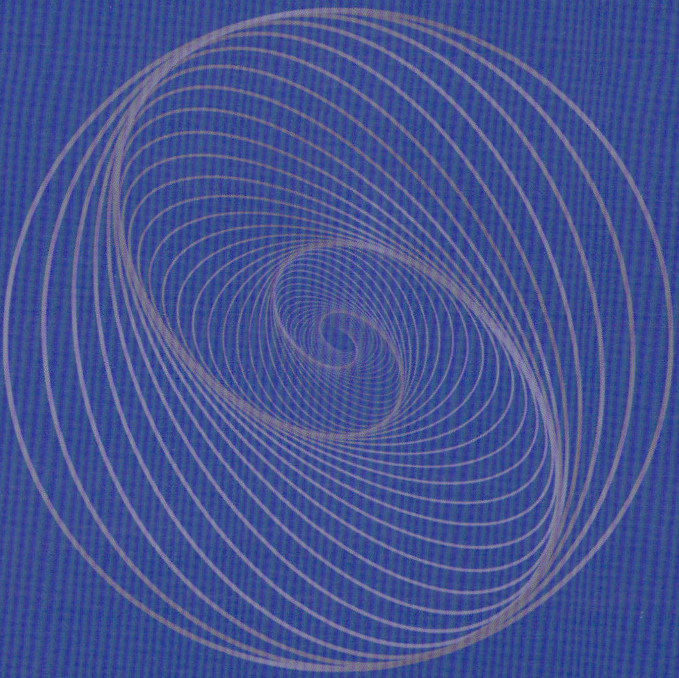

Tianjin Luban
Workshop Research
and Promotion Center

鲁班工坊
LUBAN WORKSHOP

English version

目录 CONTENTS

i

Overview

2023 marks the 10th anniversary of the Belt and Road Initiative. At the Third Belt and Road Forum for International Cooperation, President Xi Jinping said, "Luban Workshops, people-to-people exchange programs like the Silk Road Community Building Initiative and the Brightness Action program, and deepening exchanges between non-governmental organizations, think tanks, media organizations, and the youth—all these flourishing activities have composed a symphony of friendship in the new era."

As of December 2023, China has established 29 Luban Workshops in countries including Thailand, India, Indonesia, Pakistan, Cambodia, and Tajikistan in Asia; the United Kingdom, Portugal, Bulgaria, Serbia, and Russia in Europe; Djibouti, Kenya, South Africa, Mali, Nigeria, Egypt, Côte d'Ivoire, Uganda, Madagascar, Ethiopia, Morocco, Rwanda, Gabon, and Benin in Africa. An international vocational education system has been established through the Luban Workshops, spanning from secondary vocational education to higher vocational education, applied undergraduate programs, and even graduate-level studies.

According to incomplete statistics from the Tianjin Luban Workshop Research and Promotion Center, there are currently 17,600 students registered in the international cooperation programs of Luban Workshop and other elective courses. A total of 144 international enterprises have partnered with these projects.The training programs of Luban Workshop are designed for local enterprise employees in partner countries, as well as for teachers and students from partner institutions and regional schools, and the general public. The cumulative number of training participations has reached 954,000, cultivating and training a large number of urgently needed technical and skilled personnel for the economic and social development of partner countries. These workshops continue to promote the prosperity of partner countries and foster in-depth cooperation with China, becoming an important force in advancing the construction of a human community with a shared future.

After seven years of development, with the Luban Workshop serving as the platform, China and its international partners have jointly promoted the advancement and progress of vocational education. Chinese and foreign teachers have collaborated to establish international cooperation programs and develop teaching resources. To date, 145 bilingual textbooks and 420 school-based teaching materials, including self-compiled practical training lecture notes, practical training workbooks, and other materials, have been published in both Chinese and foreign languages.EPIP Research and Promotion Centers have been established in 12 countries, namely, Thailand, Indonesia, Pakistan, India, Egypt, Ethiopia, Portugal, Kenya, Kazakhstan, Uzbekistan, Madagascar, and Russia, to promote advanced teaching concepts and models. The workshops have cumulatively trained over 3,300 teachers from partner countries, with an aggregate training duration of approximately 203,200 hours.

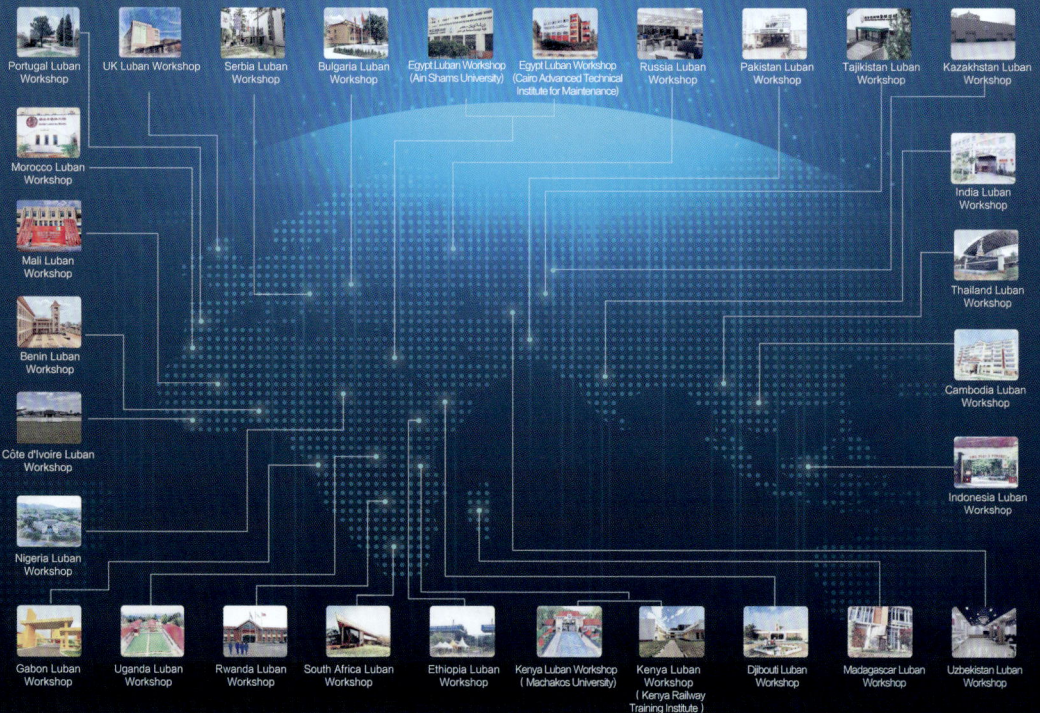

Global Distribution of Luban Workshops

Portugal Luban Workshop
UK Luban Workshop
Serbia Luban Workshop
Bulgaria Luban Workshop
Egypt Luban Workshop (Ain Shams University)
Egypt Luban Workshop (Cairo Advanced Technical Institute for Maintenance)
Russia Luban Workshop
Pakistan Luban Workshop
Tajikistan Luban Workshop
Kazakhstan Luban Workshop
Morocco Luban Workshop
India Luban Workshop
Mali Luban Workshop
Thailand Luban Workshop
Benin Luban Workshop
Cambodia Luban Workshop
Côte d'Ivoire Luban Workshop
Indonesia Luban Workshop
Nigeria Luban Workshop
Gabon Luban Workshop
Uganda Luban Workshop
Rwanda Luban Workshop
South Africa Luban Workshop
Ethiopia Luban Workshop
Kenya Luban Workshop (Machakos University)
Kenya Luban Workshop (Kenya Railway Training Institute)
Djibouti Luban Workshop
Madagascar Luban Workshop
Uzbekistan Luban Workshop

Figure 1　Global Distribution of Luban Workshops

Chapter 1
Development Process and Major Achievements

1 Pooling Resources to Achieve Leapfrog Development

In May 2023, the Second Conference of the Luban Workshop Construction Alliance was held in Tianjin. This was the first conference following the expansion of the alliance, with over 300 representatives from alliance members attending the event. Among them, 140 new institutional members and 46 new corporate members were added. As of 2023, the Luban Workshop Construction Alliance had grown to include 323 members, comprising 258 full members (200 institutional members, 54 corporate and industry association members, and four research institution members), as well as 65 institutional observers. The expansion marked a leap in the development of the alliance network.

The expansion of the alliance has provided a communication platform for more Chinese schools, enterprises, and research institutions to participate in the construction of Luban Workshops. The Second Conference featured dedicated sessions for Africa, Asia, Europe, Latin America, the Arab region, and other areas. Aiming to enhance international cooperation in vocational education across these regions, participants shared their experiences, explore various approaches, and exchange ideas on defining characteristics and strategies to address challenges in developing Luban Workshops and other overseas educational projects.Additionally, leveraging the alliance platform to pool resources and build strong synergy, efforts are made to unify perceptions and build consensus among member institutions, providing impetus for the high-standard positioning, high-level construction, and high-quality development of Luban Workshop as a flagship overseas vocational education program.

The establishment of the Luban Workshop Construction Expert Committee. The committee is composed of experts from various fields, including engineering, vocational education, international Chinese language education, and industries and enterprises. Leveraging the committee's professional expertise, it conducts specialized research and assessments to provide professional and constructive advice on the construction of Luban Workshops. This initiative aims to offer high-level professional consultation to support the high-quality development of the Luban Workshops and enhance the scientific standards of their construction efforts.

2   Launching New Projects to Support Opening Up

Vocational education cooperation projects, including the promotion of Luban Workshop construction, have been included in the list of outcomes of the China-Central Asia Summit. In May 2023, the China-Central Asia Summit proposed the implementation of the "China-Central Asia Technical and Vocational Skills Enhancement Program." This initiative aims to establish more Luban Workshops in Central Asian countries, encouraging Chinese enterprises in the region to create more local employment opportunities.

Chinese institutions have accelerated the construction of Luban Workshops in Central Asia. In August 2023, Zhejiang University of Water Resources and Electric Power, Zhejiang Vocational & Technical College of Communications, and Kyrgyz National Technical University jointly signed the Memorandum of Understanding on Luban Workshop Cooperation, marking the entry of the Kyrgyz Luban Workshop into a substantive construction phase.In December 2023, in accordance with the Regulations on Luban Workshop Construction and the Interim Standards for the Recognition of Luban Workshop Operation Projects, and following the prescribed recognition procedures, the cooperation projects between Tianjin Vocational Institute and East Kazakhstan Technical University, and between Tianjin Maritime College and Tashkent State Transport University in Uzbekistan, were recognized as Luban Workshop operation projects after joint evaluation by the China Education Association for International Exchange and the Tianjin Municipal Education Commission, and approval by the Luban Workshop Construction Alliance Council.

3   Strengthening Intellectual Property Protection to Enhance Brand Value

To strengthen international intellectual property protection for the Luban Workshop, the UK Luban Workshop initiated intellectual property protection in October 2022. After rigorous preparations, the Tianjin Academy of Educational Sciences, as the applicant, formally submitted a trademark application to the UK Intellectual Property Office in 2023. In July 2023, the Luban Workshop trademark was officially registered by the UK Intellectual Property Office under Class 41 for products and services, in accordance with standard procedures. This registration confirms that the Luban Workshop trademark is recognized by the UK government and protected under UK trademark law. The scope of protection for the Luban Workshop trademark in the UK encompasses teaching and educational services, the organization and arrangement of academic seminars, book publishing, the organization of competitions (for educational or entertainment purposes), exhibitions for cultural or educational purposes, and the production of radio and television programs, among other aspects.

The registration of the UK Luban Workshop trademark is of great significance. It marks the legal protection of a Chinese intellectual property-based vocational education brand project in an overseas partner country, effectively enhancing the brand value of the Luban Workshop as a Chinese vocational education project for international cooperation.

4   Conducting Pilot Quality Assessments to Promote Sustainable Development

Conducting quality assessments of Luban Workshops that have completed a three-year construction cycle is a systemic guarantee to ensure the high-quality and sustainable development of the projects. The Tianjin Luban Workshop Research and Promotion Center has formed an expert panel to develop a pilot version of the Luban Workshop Quality Assessment Indicator System. Drawing on the successful experience of Tianjin institutions in building Luban Workshops, the system provides a comprehensive evaluation of the Luban Workshops from multiple aspects, including overall construction quality and development capabilities

As of the end of 2023, the pilot quality assessment has been completed for eight Luban Workshop projects, including those in Thailand, the UK, Indonesia, Cambodia, India, Pakistan, Portugal, and Djibouti. The results have shown that the quality assessment plays a significant role in the sustainable development of Luban Workshops. It not only helps project teams to distill unique and innovative experiences but also provides a clear direction for the sustainable development of the projects.

5   Winning National Awards for Steering Vocational Education to Go Global

As a golden emblem of China's vocational education going global, Luban Workshop embodies the remarkable achievements of China's vocational education reform and development. To date, two of its accomplishments have been recognized with national teaching achievement awards.The project "Research and Practice: Developing Internationalized Professional Teaching Standards and Creating the Luban Workshop Vocational Education International Cooperation Projects" won the first prize of the National Teaching Achievement Award in 2018, providing pathways for deepening reform in international cooperation in vocational education.In 2022, the project "The Innovative Practices of the Luban Workshops: Model Creation, Standard Formulation, Resource Development, and Faculty Training" was awarded the special prize of the National Teaching Achievement Award. This achievement addressed the following fundamental issues in the internationalization of vocational education:

· It effectively addressed long-standing challenges in international cooperation, including blind adherence to models, dependence on external standards, and limited effectiveness.

· It systematically addressed the underlying principles for integrating industry and education, as well as for conducting transnational vocational education cooperation with a global outlook.

· It addresses the challenges of pathways, platforms, and guarantees for Chinese vocational education to expand globally and share its experiences with the world.

Chapter 2
Essence of the Program and Enhancement of Basic Capabilities

1 Scale Development of Specialties Jointly Established

With the development of the Luban Workshop Program, the scale of specialties jointly established by Chinese and foreign parties continues to expand. By 2023, a total of 76 specialties across 14 major categories have been developed, including equipment manufacturing, electronics and information technology, transportation, civil engineering and construction, energy and power materials, finance and commerce, tourism, and medical health. This represents a 15% increase compared to 2022, with higher vocational specialties accounting for 80% of the total.

The specialties offered are specifically designed to meet the needs of partner countries' economic transformation and industrial development. For instance, in Egypt, programs such as New Energy Application Technology, CNC Equipment Application and Maintenance, and Automotive Application and Repair Technology were implemented to support the country's green economy and industrial development initiatives.Similarly, in response to the demand for high-speed railway infrastructure, specialties in railway operation, maintenance, and related management were introduced in Thailand, Djibouti, and Nigeria. To meet the growing needs for information technology and intelligent technology development, specialties such as Internet of Things Application Technology and Cloud Computing have been established in countries like South Africa and Kenya, as well as in other nations⋯Advanced manufacturing technology specialties represent the category with the greatest demand across all Luban Workshops, with participating countries including Portugal, Madagascar, India, Pakistan, Uganda, and Côte d'Ivoire. This demand underscores the importance of technological advancements in the economic development of these nations.

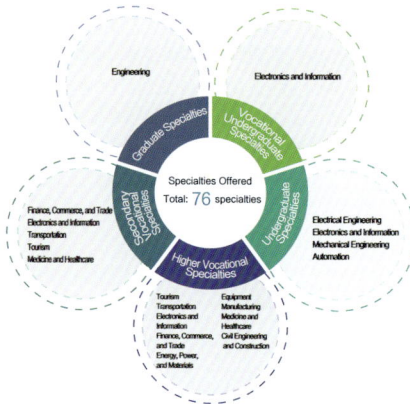

Figure 2　Overview of Specialties Offered by the Luban Workshop

2　Continuous Expansion of Educational Facilities

The educational facilities serve as the material foundation and key carrier for the smooth implementation of the Luban Workshop program. Statistical data indicate that the total area of educational facilities for the Luban Workshops has now surpassed 38,000 square meters, representing an increase of 3,832 square meters from 2022. These spaces are primarily used for professional internships and practical training, basic experimental courses, cultural exchange activities, and exhibitions showcasing project achievements.

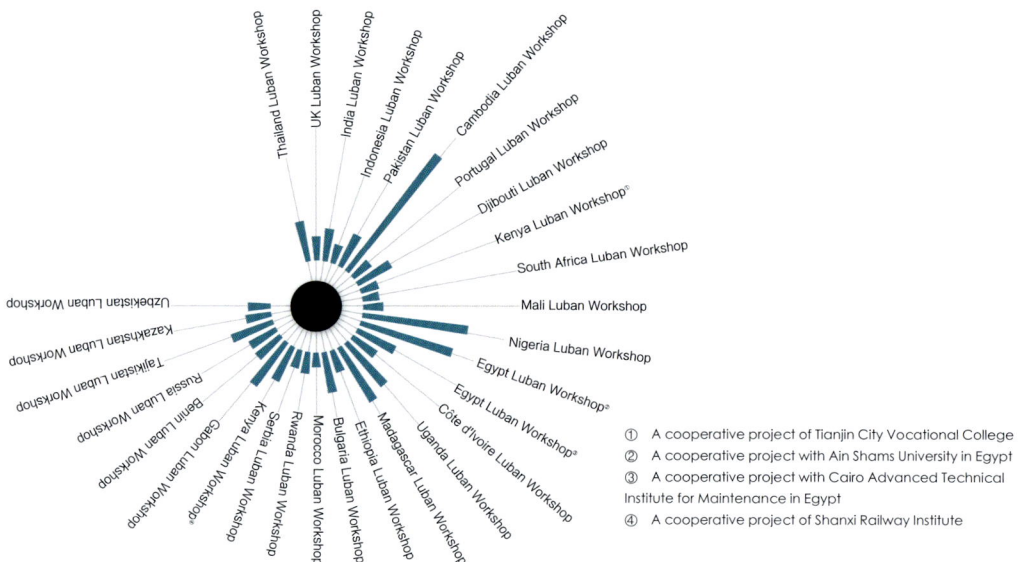

① A cooperative project of Tianjin City Vocational College
② A cooperative project with Ain Shams University in Egypt
③ A cooperative project with Cairo Advanced Technical Institute for Maintenance in Egypt
④ A cooperative project of Shanxi Railway Institute

Figure 3　Construction of Luban Workshop Facility

The facility areas of 12 Luban Workshops exceed 1,000 square meters, with the Cambodia Luban Workshop, Nigeria Luban Workshop, and Kenya Luban Workshop ranking in the top three. The Cambodia Luban Workshop, due to its role in supporting regional vocational education and training for the five Lancang–Mekong downstream countries (Myanmar, Laos, Thailand, Cambodia, and Vietnam), has 18 practical training classrooms, making its educational facility the largest in area and designed as a standalone building.

3   Ongoing Strengthening of Teaching Support

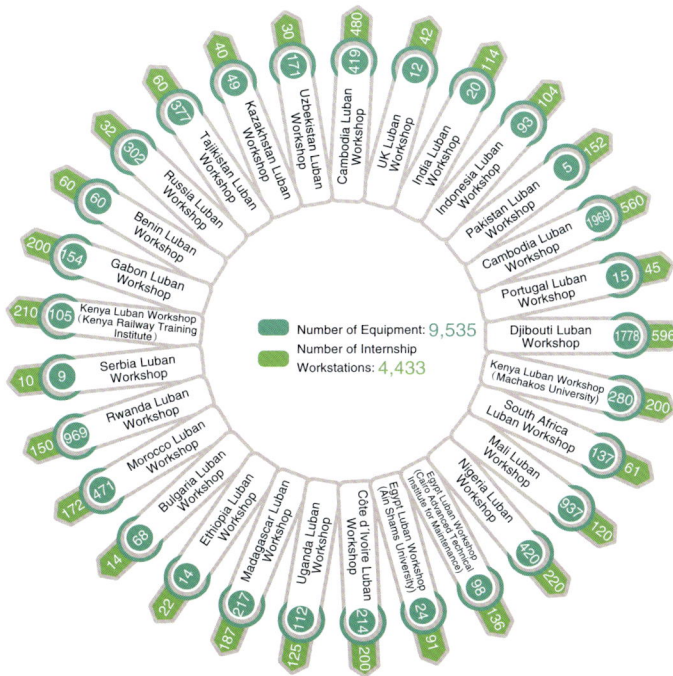

Figure 4   Teaching and Training Equipment in the Luban Workshop

Advanced teaching and training equipment is a crucial guarantee of the quality of the Luban Workshop. Across 29 projects, the total number of teaching equipment units has reached 9,535, with 1,134 units added; the total number of internship workstations available to students has increased to 4,433, with 993 workstations newly added.

This growth demonstrates that the Luban Workshop is developing rapidly through the joint efforts of Chinese and foreign participants. First, the continuous investment of resources by Chinese and foreign participants has led to an ongoing increase in the quantity of teaching equipment, as well as the updating and upgrading of technology to meet the demands of new technological developments and emerging industries. Second, the increase in the number of internship workstations indicates that the program is placing greater emphasis on cultivating students' practical skills, with the concepts of industry-education integration and school-enterprise cooperation gaining importance in partner countries. Third, the establishment of new projects and specialties shows that the Luban Workshop is continuously expanding and adapting to changes in market demand.

4   Sustained Progress in Curriculum Resource Development

First, curriculum development. Curriculum construction is the most central and critical component of the Luban Workshop. By the end of 2023, the total number of courses developed across the 29 Luban Workshops worldwide reached 534. These courses are designed based on advanced teaching models and tailored to localized needs. They are not only used for degree education in cooperative specialties but also serve as electives for other specialties, as well as for societal and corporate training. As a result, they have broad applicability and are of great significance in enhancing students' employability and promoting Sino-foreign vocational education cooperation.

Figure 5   Development of International Curriculum Resources at Luban Workshops

The scale of course development for each project is influenced by factors such as the industrial development level of the partner country, the needs of students, teachers, and trainees at the cooperating institutions, as well the requirements of degree education and vocational training systems. Consequently, the number of courses developed varies significantly across projects. The Thailand Luban Workshop, Cambodia Luban Workshop, Djibouti Luban Workshop, Rwanda Luban Workshop, and Pakistan Luban Workshop rank among the top five in terms of the number of courses developed. In terms of the categories of specialties to which these courses belong, railway operation and maintenance courses, as well as advanced manufacturing courses, have the largest scale, closely aligning with the industrial needs of the partner countries.

Second, textbook development. Textbook resources have a direct impact on the quality of teaching and learning outcomes in the Luban Workshop. By the end of 2023, the Luban Workshop had publicly published 145 bilingual textbooks in Chinese and foreign languages, while the number of institution-specific textbooks, including self-compiled training handouts and work manuals in Chinese and foreign languages, reached 420. Surveys indicate that loose-leaf institution-specific textbooks are the most widely used in the educational and teaching applications of all Luban Workshops. Their flexible format and modular content design enable customization based on students' actual conditions and needs, aligning the education and teaching of the Luban Workshop more closely with students' learning backgrounds and future career development.

Finally, the development of digital resources. With the rapid advancement of information technology, the education sector is undergoing a profound transformation. The development of digital teaching resources holds great importance for international cooperative education, as it breaks the constraints of time and space, and fully meets the professional learning needs of overseas students, teachers, and trainees from societal and corporate sectors. Statistics show that the current digital teaching resources of the Luban Workshop include PPTs (totaling 6,518), video resources (totaling 54,641.7 minutes), and question banks (totaling 967). Among the 29 projects, the top five in terms of digital resource development are the Egypt Luban Workshop, the Madagascar Luban Workshop, the Kenya Luban Workshop, the Thailand Luban Workshop, and the Mali Luban Workshop. These digital teaching resources provide strong support for the Luban Workshops to adapt to the diverse learning needs of different learners in partner countries, while also expanding the scope and forms of services offered by the Luban Workshop.

5 Establishment of a System for Overseas Teacher Training

Overseas teacher training is the primary component of the Luban Workshop initiative. Diverse training programs not only meet the needs of professional teachers to continuously improve their educational techniques and teaching methods but also lay a solid foundation for enhancing the educational quality of the Luban Workshop. Statistics show that from 2016 to 2023, the scale of training for foreign professional teachers—both in China and locally—reached 3,308 person-times. The total duration of specialized training and corporate practice courses provided for them amounted to 248,073.2 hours, with 1,654 person-times of overseas professional teachers participating in online training.

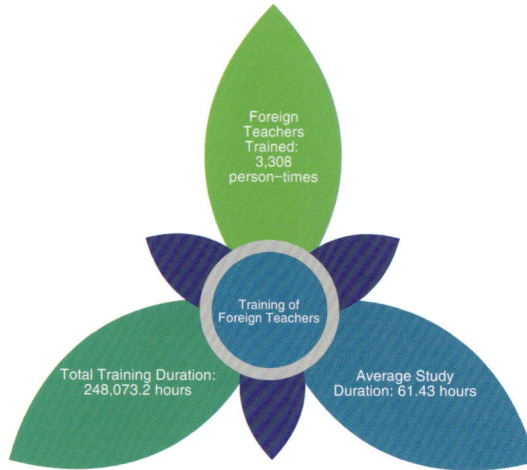

Figure 6   Training of Professional Teachers in Partner Countries

The Research and Promotion Center, through on-site interviews and investigations, found that overseas professional teachers have shown a high level of commitment to the training. They expressed that continuous training has helped them update their teaching philosophies, master new teaching methods, and broaden their international perspectives. At the same time, mutual learning and exchange with Chinese professional teachers have facilitated professional education reforms in institutions of both sides, enhancing cross-cultural communication skills. These improvements in capabilities have directly contributed to an increase in teaching quality, enabling students to receive a higher-quality education.

6   Increasing Number of Bilingual Teachers

The Luban Workshop not only shares China's outstanding educational resources and technologies with the international community but also, through the process of exchanges, significantly enhances the teaching capabilities of Chinese professional teachers, particularly in bilingual instruction. According to statistics from the Research and Promotion Center, the number of bilingual teachers in the Luban Workshop program has reached 559, with the Thailand Luban Workshop, Kenya Luban Workshop, and Rwanda Luban Workshop ranking in the top three for the number of bilingual teachers.

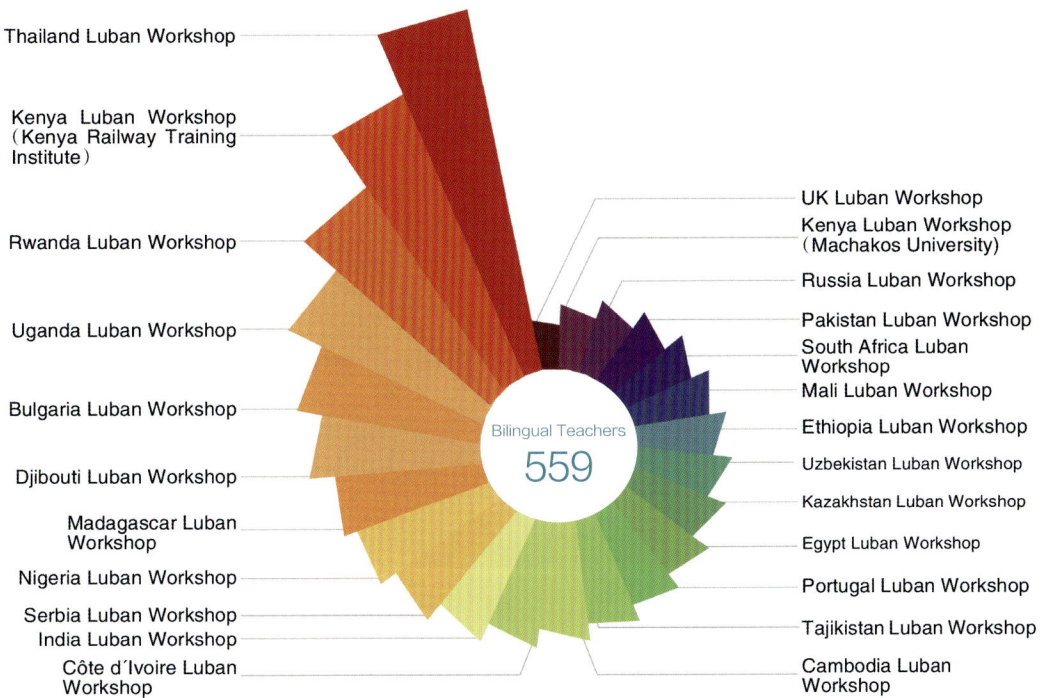

Figure 7   Overview of Bilingual Professional Teachers

Research has shown that bilingual teachers, by delivering specialized instruction proficiently in two languages, are better equipped to help students understand technical learning approaches from diverse national backgrounds, thereby fostering a global outlook among students. At the same time, bilingual teachers also shoulder the responsibility of coordinating Sino—foreign professional education and promoting cultural exchange between China and other countries. Through effective communication with educational administrators and professional teachers from various countries and regions, they assist Chinese and foreign institutions in organizing and managing the daily teaching activities of the Luban Workshop, while collaboratively developing long—term plans for its future growth and development.

Chapter 3
Talent Cultivation and Improvement of Educational and Teaching Quality

1 Scale Development of Degree Education and Professional Training

The Luban Workshop's cooperative education encompasses both degree programs and non-degree training. As of December 2023, its degree programs have served a total of 17,558 students, including those enrolled in specialized cooperative courses and electives. This figure breaks down to 570 international students studying in China and 16,988 local students in partner countries.

The number of degree-seeking students varies significantly across countries, influenced by factors such as local education policies and the demand for industrial development. Certain countries, including Tajikistan, India, Cambodia, Egypt, Côte d'Ivoire, Uganda, and Ethiopia—spanning Asia and Africa—tend to have higher numbers of students in degree programs. As of December 2023, the Luban Workshop's total enrollment stands at 11,371 students. Chinese and foreign professional teachers have collaborated to design comprehensive curricula, enabling students to receive a well-rounded education in knowledge and skills, covering foundational professional theory and integrated practical courses.

The diverse vocational training programs offered by the Luban Workshop play a key role in helping countries enhance their human resource capabilities and boost economic growth. According to statistics from the Research and Promotion Center, the Luban Workshop has provided training for a total of 95,421 person-times. This includes 7,429 person-times of customized training for company employees and 87,992 person-times for the broader community, including teachers, students, and societal trainees. These efforts underscore the Luban Workshop's commitment to social responsibility, as it provides corporate and community training to upskill local workers and support the social and economic development of its partner countries.

Figure 8: Talent Cultivation of the Luban Workshop

Figure 9   Overview of Training at Luban Workshop

The Luban Workshop's non-degree education offers vocational training, short-term courses, and workshops, providing working professionals with opportunities to upskill and update their knowledge and skills. By blending online and offline methods, it leverages information technology to deliver targeted training services to a wider audience of company employees and community members. This flexible and adaptable approach meets the diverse technical skill training needs of partner countries. Statistics reveal significant variations in the scale of non-degree training across different countries and regions. Thailand, India, and Djibouti stand out with higher numbers of training person-times, with Thailand leading by a wide margin. Its influence extends beyond regional and national boundaries, establishing a notable presence within ASEAN.Years of practice show that while information technology greatly expands the reach of training, it also poses quality challenges, as it doesn't always guarantee the same effectiveness as traditional in-person training. Addressing this issue remains a key focus for future training efforts.

2   Steady Improvement of Talent Cultivation Quality[1]

The Luban Workshop initiative goes beyond preparing students for employment; it also supports their personal growth and career planning. Since the first cohort graduated in

[1]   This is a research outcome of the National Social Science Fund Youth Project titled "Research on Promoting China's Leadership in Building a Global Vocational Education Governance System Based on the 'Luban Workshop' under the New 'Dual Circulation' Paradigm" (Project No. 21CGL042).

15

2018, more than 6,000 degree-seeking students have completed their programs at Luban Workshops worldwide by 2023. Some graduates secure jobs with local companies in partner countries, while others pursue further education. Influenced by external factors and data availability, incomplete statistics from the Tianjin Luban Workshop Research and Promotion Center indicate that 3,263 graduates have found local employment. These graduates, equipped with high-quality degree education and vocational training, possess advanced industry skills, proficiency with technical equipment, and some research and development capabilities. This makes them highly competitive young professionals in their respective regions, a result particularly evident in fast-growing economies such as Indonesia and Pakistan. Surveys show that another group of graduates advances to higher education through national exams, with diverse pathways including transitions from secondary vocational schools to higher vocational institutions, from higher vocational programs to applied undergraduate programs, and from undergraduate studies to graduate programs.

Teacher and Student Satisfaction Survey. The cultivation of highly skilled technical talent lies at the heart of the global Luban Workshop initiative. Overall, after seven years of high-quality development and steady progress, the Luban Workshop has achieved remarkable success in talent cultivation.First, both teachers and students highly approve of the entire talent cultivation process at the Luban Workshops. They agree that the program's goals meet diverse needs, with 88.14% of teachers and 86.24% of students affirming that these goals align with student development needs— the highest-rated aspect. Additionally, 88.18% of Luban Workshop students express satisfaction with the teaching methods. Regarding the effectiveness of talent cultivation, students believe multiple factors influence their future career prospects. The top three factors they identify are: alignment of specialties with industry needs (73.26%), rich and practical course content (67.25%), and strong teacher capabilities paired with effective learning outcomes (62.98%). Students also show a clear inclination toward China in their aspirations, with 36.24% aiming for employment and 45.74% pursuing further studies there. Moreover, 83.92% of students believe the Luban Workshop is highly popular locally, establishing it as a vital project that enhances livelihoods. Second, graduates report high satisfaction with their academic achievements. Through the Luban Workshop's training, graduates report significant gains in five key competencies: information acquisition and application (76.54%), interpersonal skills (72.63%), technical application (65.92%), resource management (56.42%), and coordination (28.49%). Third, graduates express positive feedback about their employment satisfaction. Overall, 87.15% of Luban Workshop graduates are satisfied with their jobs, with 91.62% fully adapting to their workplace environments and 92.74% believe their Luban Workshop experience has expanded their future career opportunities. The survey ultimately reveals that 91.62% of graduates strongly recommend the Luban Workshop.

（1） Both Teachers and Students Highly Approve of the Entire Talent Cultivation Process at the Luban Workshops

Frontline teachers and students of the Luban Workshop overwhelmingly endorse its efforts in three key areas: the design of specialties and training objectives, the organization and delivery of teaching, and the outcomes of talent cultivation.

First, Design of Specialties and Talent Cultivation Objectives, both frontline teachers and students agree that the Luban Workshop's talent cultivation objectives effectively address diverse needs. Among these, the highest-rated aspect is its ability to meet student development needs, with 88.14% of teachers and 86.24% of students affirming this (see Figures 10 and 11). The data highlights that the Luban Workshop's development prioritizes students, with both teachers and students placing student development needs at the forefront. A comparative analysis shows that their evaluations of the talent cultivation objectives are largely aligned.

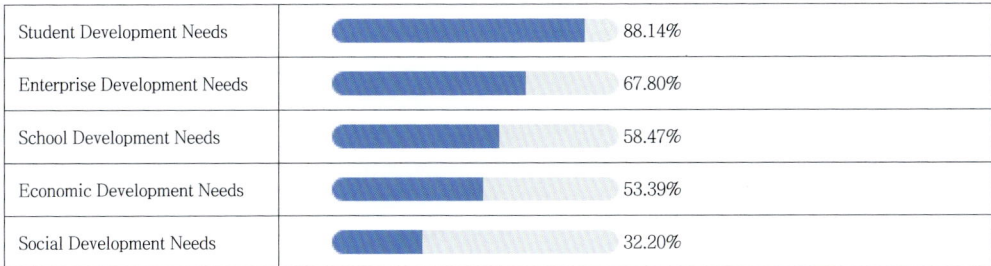

Student Development Needs	88.14%
Enterprise Development Needs	67.80%
School Development Needs	58.47%
Economic Development Needs	53.39%
Social Development Needs	32.20%

Figure 10   Teachers' evaluation of how effectively talent cultivation objectives meet diverse needs.

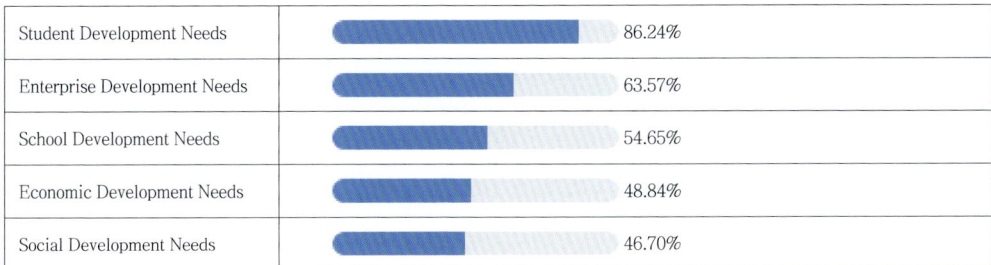

Student Development Needs	86.24%
Enterprise Development Needs	63.57%
School Development Needs	54.65%
Economic Development Needs	48.84%
Social Development Needs	46.70%

Figure 11   Students' evaluation of how effectively talent cultivation objectives meet diverse needs.

Second, Teaching Organization and Implementation，in terms of teaching content, the curriculum is the cornerstone. According to student surveys, Luban Workshop students express high satisfaction with the curriculum design. The top four aspects they appreciate most are: strong practicality of courses (79.26%), reasonable course content (51.94%), well-designed course scheduling (50.19%), and a balanced ratio of theoretical to practical courses (50.00%) (see Figure 12). This data indicates that the Luban Workshop aims to train high-quality workers and skilled technical talent for partner countries, placing a strong emphasis on the practicality of its curriculum—a factor that students rate as the most satisfying aspect of the curriculum design.

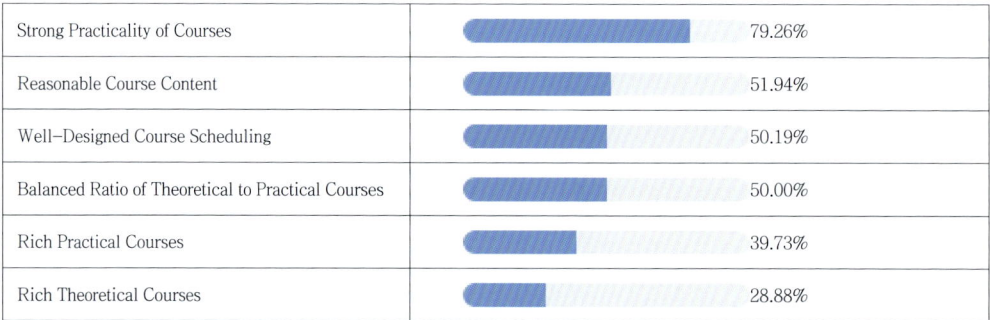

Strong Practicality of Courses	79.26%
Reasonable Course Content	51.94%
Well-Designed Course Scheduling	50.19%
Balanced Ratio of Theoretical to Practical Courses	50.00%
Rich Practical Courses	39.73%
Rich Theoretical Courses	28.88%

Figure 12　Students' Evaluation of Curriculum Design

Regarding teaching methods, 79.67% of frontline teachers believe they can proficiently apply the EPIP teaching approach in their instruction (see Figure 13), while 88.18% of Luban Workshop students are satisfied with the teaching methods (see Figure 14).

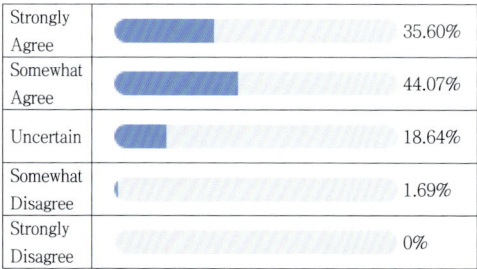

Strongly Agree	35.60%
Somewhat Agree	44.07%
Uncertain	18.64%
Somewhat Disagree	1.69%
Strongly Disagree	0%

Strongly Agree	64.15%
Somewhat Agree	24.03%
Uncertain	8.33%
Somewhat Disagree	2.52%
Strongly Disagree	0.97%

Figure 13　Teachers' Evaluation of Their Ability to Proficiently Apply the EPIP Teaching Approach

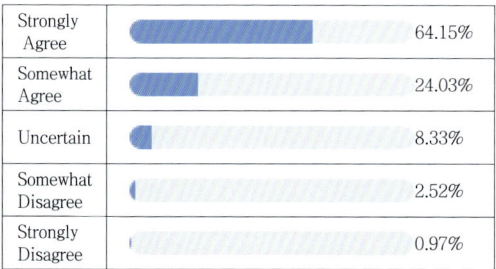

Figure 14　Students' Evaluation of Their Satisfaction with the Teaching Methods

In terms of teaching resources, students at the Luban Workshop rate teaching equipment (85.85%), bilingual textbooks (77.91%), and online courses (74.22%) as the top three most satisfying aspects (see Figure 15). The data suggests that, compared to the "soft" resources in the Luban Workshop's resource development, "hard" resources like teaching equipment tend to earn higher satisfaction from students.

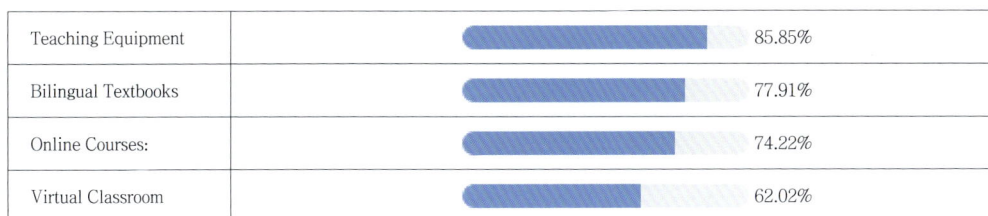

Teaching Equipment	85.85%
Bilingual Textbooks	77.91%
Online Courses:	74.22%
Virtual Classroom	62.02%

Figure 15   Students' Evaluation of Teaching Resources

Luban Workshop students give positive feedback on the teaching abilities of their instructors. They highlight a professional teaching attitude (73.45%), effective teaching outcomes (58.33%), and diverse teaching methods (55.23%) as the top three aspects of instructors' performance that satisfy them most (see Figure 16). The data indicates that in evaluations of teaching quality at the Luban Workshop, frontline teachers demonstrate significant care and support for students, making their professional attitude the most appreciated aspect among students.

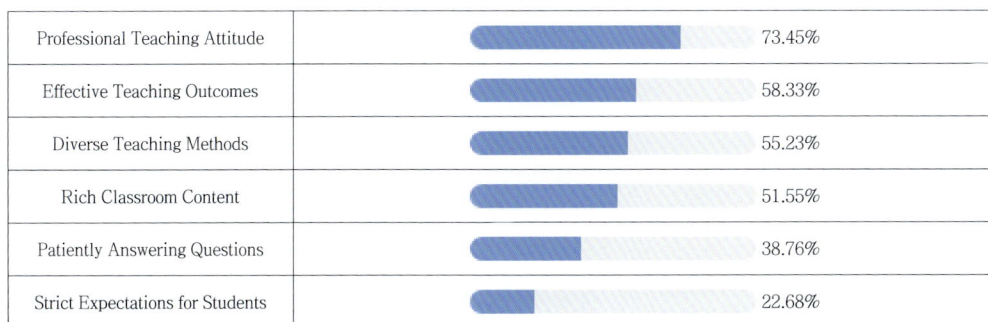

Professional Teaching Attitude	73.45%
Effective Teaching Outcomes	58.33%
Diverse Teaching Methods	55.23%
Rich Classroom Content	51.55%
Patiently Answering Questions	38.76%
Strict Expectations for Students	22.68%

Figure 16   Students' Evaluation of Instructors' Teaching Abilities

In terms of teacher training, among the frontline teachers surveyed at Luban Workshops, all of them have undergone teacher training specific to Luban Workshop, though the locations and instructors varied. Of these, 26.27% received training in China,

27.97% were trained in their home country by Chinese instructors, and 45.76% were trained in their home country by local instructors (see Figure 17). The data shows that the majority of frontline teachers at Luban Workshops received their teaching training in their home country. Moving forward, there is a need to increase the proportion of frontline teachers coming to China for training to further enhance the quality of teaching.

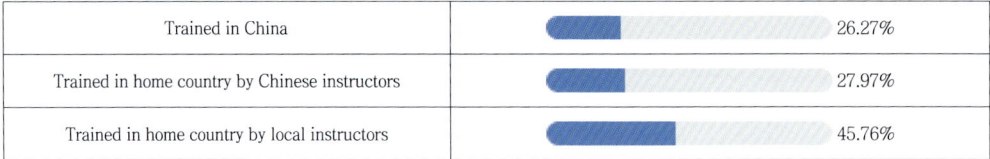

Trained in China	26.27%
Trained in home country by Chinese instructors	27.97%
Trained in home country by local instructors	45.76%

Figure 17   Teachers Training

Third, Outcomes of Talent Cultivation，in terms of teaching effectiveness, frontline teachers identify advanced teaching equipment (86.44%), suitable teaching materials (65.25%), and clear teaching objectives (60.17%) as the three primary factors influencing the Luban Workshop's teaching outcomes (see Figure 18). The data underscores that, as one of the key elements of the "Five Readiness" framework, having "equipment in place" plays a significant role in enhancing teaching effectiveness.

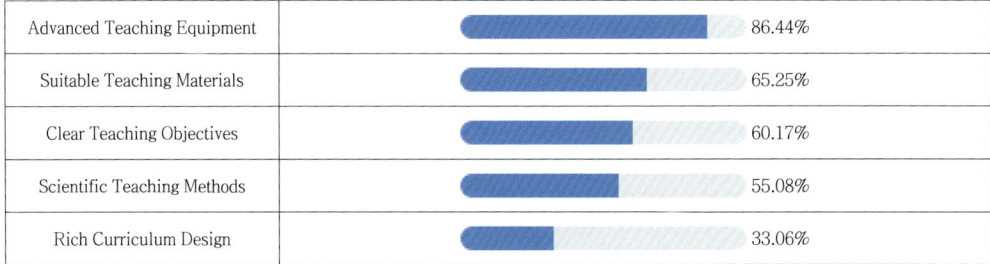

Advanced Teaching Equipment	86.44%
Suitable Teaching Materials	65.25%
Clear Teaching Objectives	60.17%
Scientific Teaching Methods	55.08%
Rich Curriculum Design	33.06%

Figure 18   Teachers' Evaluation of Factors Influencing Teaching Effectiveness

The primary paths for Luban Workshop graduates are employment and further education. One of the key goals of vocational education is to enable students to secure high-quality jobs. In student surveys, Luban Workshop students identified multiple factors influencing their future career development. The top three they consider most significant are: specialties aligned with enterprise needs (73.26%), rich and practical course content (67.25%), and strong teacher capabilities paired with effective learning outcomes (62.98%) (see Figure 19). The data highlights that the Luban Workshop deeply supports international industrial capacity cooperation. Through industry-education integration and school-enterprise partnerships, it provides technical and skilled talent to partner countries, facilitating their industrial transformation and upgrading. As a result, the alignment of specialties with enterprise needs stands out as the most critical factor affecting students' career development.

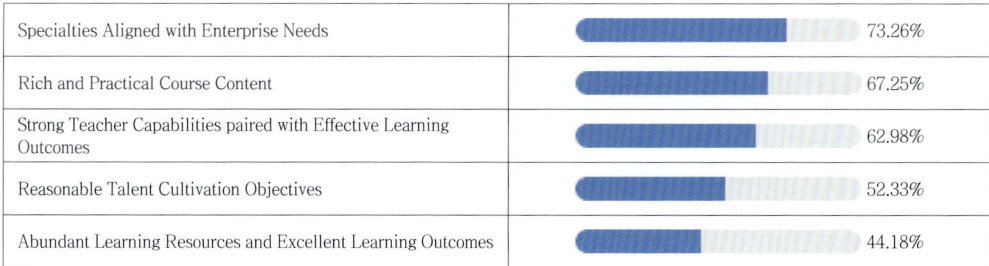

Specialties Aligned with Enterprise Needs	73.26%
Rich and Practical Course Content	67.25%
Strong Teacher Capabilities paired with Effective Learning Outcomes	62.98%
Reasonable Talent Cultivation Objectives	52.33%
Abundant Learning Resources and Excellent Learning Outcomes	44.18%

Figure 19 Students' Evaluation of Factors Influencing Career Development

Regarding future employment expectations, 36.24% of Luban Workshop students aspire to work at Chinese-funded enterprises, 22.48% aim to join domestic companies in their home countries, and 20.54% hope to work at joint-venture firms (see Figure 20). The data shows that employment at Chinese-funded enterprises is the top career aspiration among Luban Workshop students.

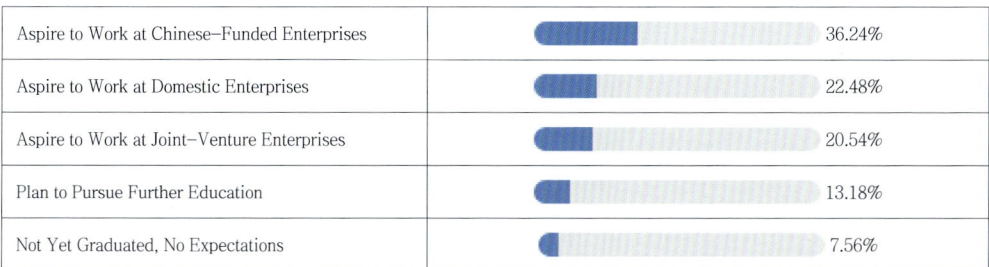

Aspire to Work at Chinese-Funded Enterprises	36.24%
Aspire to Work at Domestic Enterprises	22.48%
Aspire to Work at Joint-Venture Enterprises	20.54%
Plan to Pursue Further Education	13.18%
Not Yet Graduated, No Expectations	7.56%

Figure 20 Students' Expectations for Future Employment

The desire to pursue further education among Luban Workshop students also reflects an inclination toward China. Surveys show that 45.74% of students wish to continue their studies in China, 32.75% prefer to study further in their home countries, 15.89% aim to attend schools in countries other than China or their home nation, and 5.62% have no intention of pursuing further education (see Figure 21). The data indicates that continuing education in China is the top aspiration for Luban Workshop students.

Aspire to Continue Studying in China		45.74%
Aspire to Continue Studying in Their Home Country		32.75%
Aspire to Continue Studying in Other Countries (Not China or Home Country)		15.89%
No Intention to Pursue Further Education		5.62%

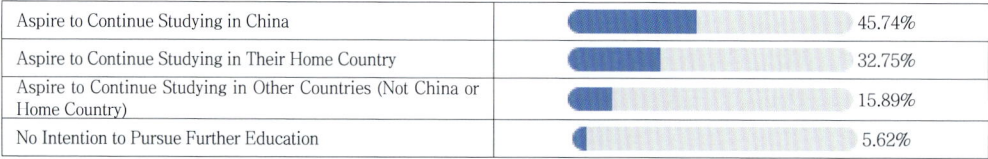

Figure 21　Students' Intentions for Further Education

In evaluating the local popularity of the Luban Workshop, 58.53% of students strongly agree that it is well-received, and 25.39% somewhat agree, together accounting for 83.92% of all surveyed students (see Figure 22). The data confirms that the Luban Workshop enjoys strong local popularity and stands as a vital livelihood-enhancing project.

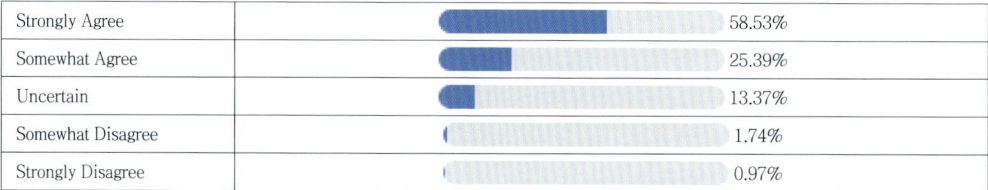

Strongly Agree		58.53%
Somewhat Agree		25.39%
Uncertain		13.37%
Somewhat Disagree		1.74%
Strongly Disagree		0.97%

Figure 22　Students' Evaluation of Its Local Popularity

（2） High Satisfaction in Talent Cultivation and Academic Achievement Among Luban Workshop Graduates

First, Luban Workshop Graduates Rate Talent Cultivation Highly.Luban Workshop graduates express strong satisfaction with the talent cultivation process. Specifically, 74.30% value the practicality of internships and training, 70.95% find the course content well-designed, 69.27% praise the strong teaching abilities of instructors, 50.28% appreciate the variety of teaching methods, and 35.20% consider the teaching resources abundant (see Figure 23). The data reveals that the practicality of internships and training is the aspect of talent cultivation that graduates are most satisfied with, aligning with current students' top satisfaction factor— the strong practicality of the curriculum.

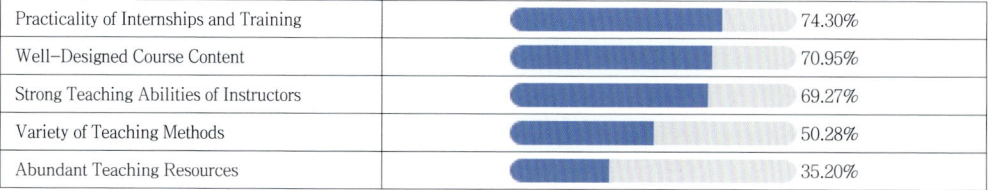

Practicality of Internships and Training		74.30%
Well-Designed Course Content		70.95%
Strong Teaching Abilities of Instructors		69.27%
Variety of Teaching Methods		50.28%
Abundant Teaching Resources		35.20%

Figure 23　Graduates' Evaluation of Talent Cultivation

Second, Luban Workshop Graduates Highly Rate Their Academic Achievement Satisfaction Overall, through the Luban Workshop's talent cultivation, graduates report a strong sense of achievement in five key competencies: information acquisition and application (76.54%), interpersonal skills (72.63%), technical application (65.92%), resource management (56.42%), and coordination (28.49%) (see Figure 24). The data suggests that in the digital era, graduates feel the greatest sense of accomplishment in their ability to acquire and apply information.

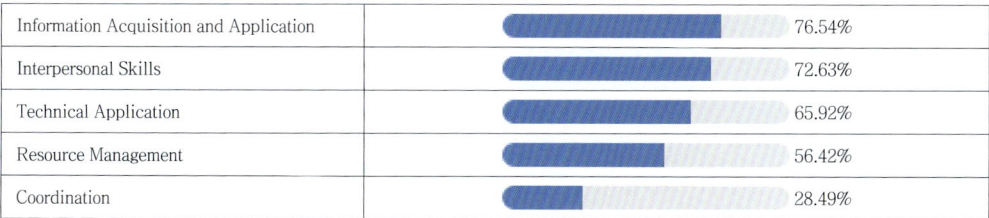

Information Acquisition and Application		76.54%
Interpersonal Skills		72.63%
Technical Application		65.92%
Resource Management		56.42%
Coordination		28.49%

Figure 24　Graduates' Evaluation of Competency Gains

（3） Luban Workshop Graduates Give Positive Feedback on Employment Satisfaction

Luban Workshop graduates report high levels of job satisfaction. Overall, 87.15% of graduates are satisfied with their work (see Figure 25).

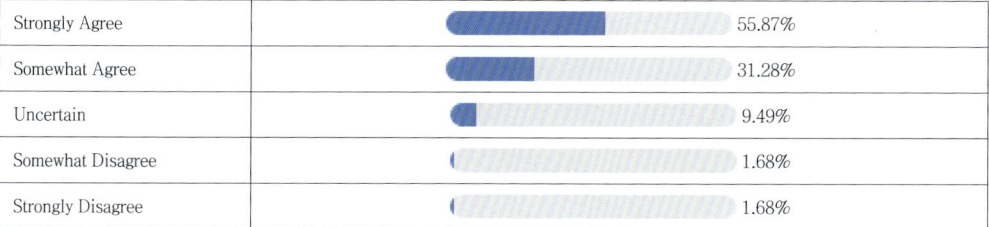

Strongly Agree		55.87%
Somewhat Agree		31.28%
Uncertain		9.49%
Somewhat Disagree		1.68%
Strongly Disagree		1.68%

Figure 25　Graduates' Evaluation of Overall Job Satisfaction

In terms of workplace adaptability, an impressive 91.62% of Luban Workshop graduates report being fully able to adjust to their work environment (see Figure 26). Regarding future career prospects, 92.74% believe that their Luban Workshop experience helps expand their opportunities for career development (see Figure 27).

Fully Able	73.74%
Somewhat Able	17.88%
Uncertain	6.15%
Somewhat Unable	0%
Completely Unable	2.23%

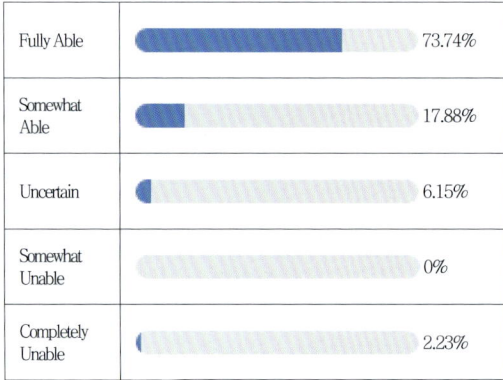

Figure 26　Graduates' Evaluation of Their Ability to Adapt to the Work Environment

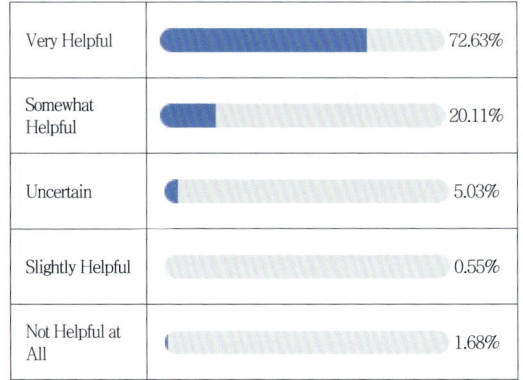

Very Helpful	72.63%
Somewhat Helpful	20.11%
Uncertain	5.03%
Slightly Helpful	0.55%
Not Helpful at All	1.68%

Figure 27　Graduates' Evaluation of Whether Their Experience Benefits Career Development

The survey ultimately reveals that an impressive 91.62% of Luban Workshop graduates are highly likely to recommend the program, with 74.86% very willing and 16.76% somewhat willing (see Figure 28). The data confirms that the Luban Workshop has become a vital livelihood-enhancing project, earning widespread praise from local students.

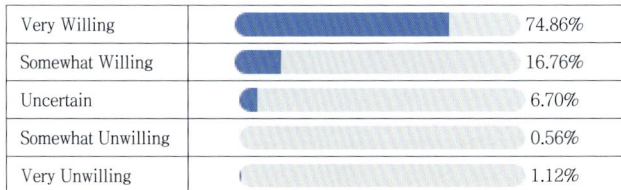

Very Willing	74.86%
Somewhat Willing	16.76%
Uncertain	6.70%
Somewhat Unwilling	0.56%
Very Unwilling	1.12%

Figure 28　Graduates' Evaluation of Whether They Would Recommend the Program to Friends and Family

Chapter 4
Enhanced Influence through Deepening Cooperation and Exchange

1 Chinese and Foreign Teachers and Students Jointly Participating in Skills Competitions

Thanks to its high-quality education and teaching, faculty and students from the Chinese and foreign partner institutions of the Luban Workshop have achieved outstanding results in various domestic and international skills competitions, with the number of awards increasing year by year, particularly in the form of gold medals. Collectively, Chinese and foreign teachers and students have won a total of 1,550 awards across all levels of competitions, with teachers earning 1,014 awards and students securing 536.

The skills competitions span a wide range. International events include the inaugural World Vocational College Skills Competition, the Belt and Road & BRICS Skills Development and Technology Innovation Competition, the China International College Students' "Internet+" Innovation and Entrepreneurship Competition, and the ASEAN Skills Competition. At the national level, technical skills contests include the National Vocational College Skills Competition (China), the Russia "Information Technology in Complex Systems" Internet Olympiad, the Tajikistan "Science – Light of Knowledge" Competition, the Thailand Vocational Skills Competition, the Indonesia National Automated Production Line Competition, and the Qicheng Cup 4th China EPIP Micromouse International Invitational & China Regional Selection for the International Computer Competition. In these global and regional technical skills contests, participants from Luban Workshop partner institutions have excelled, with a steady rise in gold medal wins. These honors and achievements not only highlight the Luban Workshop's remarkable success in cultivating internationally competitive skilled talent but also lay a strong foundation for future Sino-foreign educational collaboration.

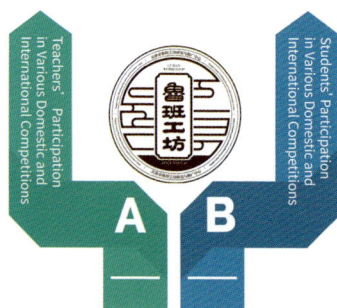

A

1. World Vocational College Skills Competition
2. World Robot Contest Championship
3. BRICS Vocational Skills Competition
4. Belt and Road & BRICS Skills Development and Technology Innovation Competition
5. National Vocational College Teachers' Skills Competition
6. National Industry Vocational Skills Competition
7. National Digital Creativity Teaching Skills Competition
8. National Artificial Intelligence Application Technology Skills Competition
9. National Vocational Skills Competition
10. International Invitational of the National Vocational College Skills Competition
11. Qicheng Cup EPIP Luban Workshop International Invitational
12. International Division of the Machinery Industry Vocational Education Skills Competition
13. Engineering Practice Innovation Project Teacher-Student Challenge

B

1. World Vocational College Skills Competition
2. Belt and Road & BRICS Skills Development and Technology Innovation Competition
3. International Smart Sports Conference
4. China-Africa (Ethiopia) University Students' Industrial Robot Technology Application Friendship Competition
5. Thailand Vocational and Basic Skills Competition
6. Thailand Inaugural Railway Transport System Invitational
7. Djibouti Luban Workshop Vocational Skills Competition
8. Qicheng Cup EPIP Luban Workshop International Invitational
9. Qicheng Cup Micromouse International Invitational
10. Russia "Information Technology in Complex Systems" Internet Olympiad
11. Russia Computer Security Competition
12. Russia 6th National Inter-University Student Championship
13. Tajikistan "Science - Light of Knowledge" Competition
14. Indonesia Skills Competition

Figure 29　Participation of Luban Workshop Teachers and Students in Various Skills Competitions

2　Chinese and Foreign Participating Institutions Winning Government Awards

The international influence of the Luban Workshop is immense, earning high recognition from both Chinese and foreign governments. On one hand, to honor the project's significant contributions to local social and economic development, partner country governments have bestowed various awards on the Chinese institutions involved in the Luban Workshop initiative. Notable examples include:

· Tianjin Bohai Vocational Technical College and Tianjin Railway Vocational and Technical College, the Chinese partners of the Thailand Luban Workshop, which received the Princess Sirindhorn Commemorative Medal, the Outstanding Contribution Award from the Thai Vocational Education Commission, and the Outstanding Contribution Award from the Ayutthaya Provincial Government.

· Zhongde University of Applied Sciences, the Chinese partner of the Cambodia Luban Workshop, was awarded the Sahametrei Officer and Knight Medal by the Cambodian government, as well as the Outstanding Contribution Award from the Cambodian Ministry of Labor.

· Zhejiang Tourism Vocational College, the Chinese partner of the Serbia Luban Workshop, which received the Excellence Award from the World Federation of Colleges and Polytechnics (WFCP).

On the other hand, the Chinese government has also highly commended foreign institutions for their exceptional contributions. For instance, the former president of Ayutthaya Technical College in Thailand, recognized for his pivotal role in establishing and developing the first Luban Workshop, advancing Sino-Thai cultural exchange, and promoting international industry-education collaboration, was honored with the Chinese Government Friendship Award in 2023.

3   Hosting Diverse Cultural Exchange Activities

Promoting cultural exchange between China and other countries is one of the core missions of the Luban Workshop. Key forms of this exchange include mutual visits by teachers and students, joint Sino-foreign teams competing in contests, and hosting academic forums. These diverse approaches transcend geographical barriers, creating a platform for interaction among teachers, students, officials, scholars, and entrepreneurs from different nations. By the end of 2023, the total volume of Sino-foreign teacher and student exchanges reached 8,216 person-times. Offline exchanges included 741 person-times of student-to-student visits and 1,589 person-times of teacher-to-teacher visits, with the remainder conducted online. Additionally, 1,200 person-times of Chinese and foreign teachers and students participated in exchanges through various technical skills competitions, including 131 person-times of professional teachers and 1,069 person-times of students.

In 2023, the "Belt and Road Vocational Education International Cooperation and Development Forum" was held in Portugal. Attendees included representatives from Portuguese higher education departments, government officials from Setúbal, delegates from the Chinese and foreign partner institutions of the Portugal Luban Workshop, representatives from Portuguese-speaking partner universities, and experts from the Tianjin Academy of Educational Sciences. Under the theme "Innovation, Integration, Development," they explored how international projects can drive Sino-Portuguese cooperation and exchange. Chinese and foreign experts proposed strengthening collaboration in two areas: First, enhancing research and educational cooperation in applied technology fields fosters Sino-foreign teacher and student exchanges, creates a diverse international educational environment for students, and promotes mutual understanding and progress across borders. Second, establishing a Portugal Luban Workshop School-Enterprise Alliance, leveraging advanced technical equipment to deepen ties with international enterprises, and offering tailored solutions to achieve mutual benefits.

4 Projects Attracting Global Attention from Chinese and Foreign Media

Since its inception, the Luban Workshop initiative has garnered significant attention from governments and social organizations worldwide, with sustained coverage from both Chinese and foreign media. According to incomplete statistics from the Research and Promotion Center, the total number of reports in authoritative domestic and international media has reached 2,067 as of the current date.

Traditional and new media outlets—such as Thailand's Siam Rath Online News and Daily News, the UK's BBC, India's Trinity Mirror, Cambodia's Koh Santepheap and Phnom Penh TV, Portugal's CISION, Conta Loios, Wintech, PCGUIA, and SAPO portal, Djibouti National Television, Djibouti National Newspaper, and South Africa's SABC—have provided ongoing coverage of the Luban Workshop's establishment and growth. Today, an increasing number of partner countries value the construction and development of the Luban Workshop, viewing it as a bridge of friendship that fosters mutual understanding with the Chinese people.

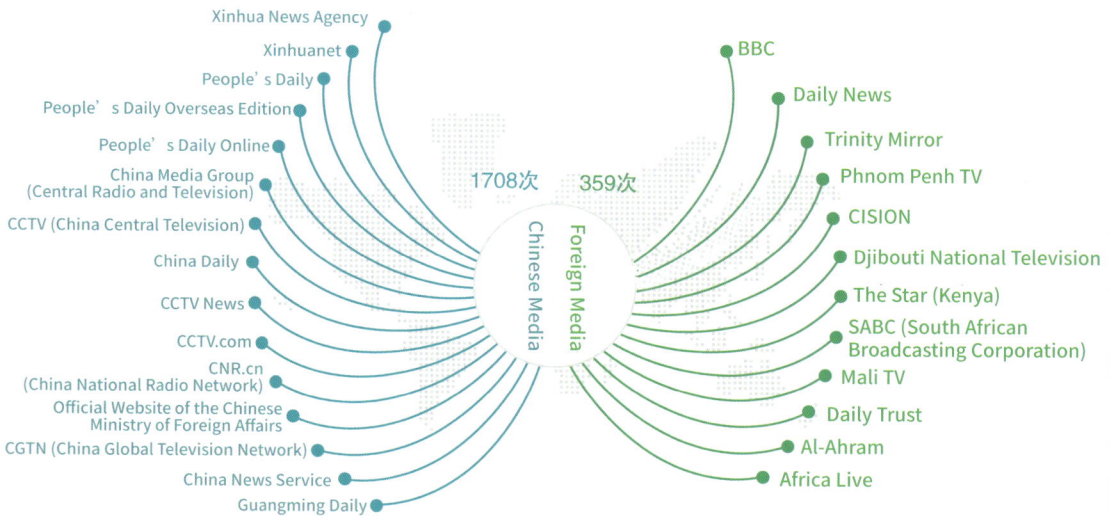

Figure 30   Global Media Coverage of the Luban Workshop

Chapter 5
Deepening Industry-Education Integration to Promote Regional Development

1 Serving the Higher-Quality and Intensive Development of Enterprises

Implementing international industry-education integration is a core component of the Luban Workshop's efforts to support global production capacity cooperation and a fundamental principle guiding its establishment and development. As the labor market becomes increasingly globalized, the flow and migration of technical and skilled talent worldwide have become an inevitable trend, creating an urgent need to strengthen industry-education integration and school-enterprise collaboration to advance technological development across nations. This approach not only serves as a vital pathway for boosting local economies and international production-capacity cooperation but also stands as an effective means for vocational education worldwide to achieve high-quality development.

China has signed Belt and Road cooperation agreements with over 80 countries, established an institutionalized production-capacity cooperation mechanism with more than 30 nations, and promoted the development of 75 overseas economic and trade cooperation zones in 24 partner countries. These efforts have created nearly 200,000 jobs, exerting a positive and far-reaching impact on global development. Whether through the Belt and Road international production capacity cooperation or the Luban Workshop's contributions to industrial growth in host countries, there is a pressing need to accelerate vocational education and train high-quality, localized talent to provide the human resources necessary for sustaining global economic growth.

By the end of 2023, the Luban Workshop had provided training to a total of 95,400 person-times for various enterprises and communities. The training programs are diverse, encompassing customized specialized programs and community training, delivered through both in-person sessions and online platforms. To date, the cumulative scale of online training has reached 13,699 person-times, with the scope of services continuing to expand. The 29 Luban Workshops annually train over

10,000 degree-seeking students urgently needed in their regions, spanning four educational levels: secondary vocational, higher vocational, applied undergraduate, and graduate. This effectively meets the pressing demand of local enterprises for skilled technical talent in critical specialties, as well as the vocational training needs of teachers, students, and community members in the host regions.

The primary objective of international industry-education integration and school-enterprise cooperation is to support the social and economic development of partner countries and regions. The Luban Workshop's development closely aligns with the socioeconomic plans and industrial upgrading needs of two or more countries in a region, supporting their progress through diverse means such as talent cultivation and technical innovation. Surveys indicate that international school-enterprise collaboration within the Luban Workshop framework is deeply integrated. Partner enterprises actively participate in its establishment and development, embedding their technical standards and processes into every stage of the educational process—from designing specialty standards to developing course resources, and organizing and delivering instruction. This ensures that the Luban Workshop's education and teaching fully align with the practical demands of international socioeconomic development, producing competitive, localized technical and skilled talent.

2 Typical Case Analysis of Serving Industrial Development

Case Study 1

Fueling Regional Collaborative Development

A prime example is the Cambodia Luban Workshop, established to support Lancang-Mekong Cooperation. It is positioned to be based in Cambodia, serving the five Lancang-Mekong downstream countries, and extending its reach to all ten ASEAN nations. This workshop integrates vocational education, vocational training, scientific research, cultural preservation, and innovation and entrepreneurship into a market-oriented, international vocational education center.

Case Study 2

Supporting Africa's Railway and Transit Industry Development

Take Tianjin Railway Vocational and Technical College as an example. Since the establishment of the Djibouti Luban Workshop and Nigeria Luban Workshop in 2019, they have provided online training for local employees of the Addis Ababa-Djibouti Railway in eight specialties, including track workers, signal technicians, and communication technicians. A total of 2,967 local employees have earned certificates for completing their training. From 2022 to 2023, the workshops completed training for railway staff at the Nagad Station and senior managers of the Addis Ababa-Djibouti Railway, offering critical support for the railway's localized operations in Africa on the 10th anniversary of the Belt and Road Initiative.

Case Study 3

Serving Agricultural Technology Development in South Asia

A notable case is the Pakistan Luban Workshop, designed to support the development of industrial modern technology talent and the mechanized transformation of agriculture in Punjab, Pakistan's "super province." In collaboration with the international enterprise Yongmeng Machinery Co., Ltd., the project partners have tailored their efforts to Pakistan's agricultural development needs. They have developed relevant course standards and designed agricultural machinery, promoting the application and innovation of mechanized farming in their local area. With powerful, high-performance, and smart agricultural equipment, their technology has gained widespread recognition in Pakistan.

Chapter 6
Strategies for Building and Developing an International Brand

At the Beijing Summit of the Forum on China-Africa Cooperation on September 3, 2018, China announced the establishment of 10 Luban Workshops in Africa to train African youth in vocational skills. On October 18, 2023, the Third Belt and Road Forum for International Cooperation unveiled eight actions for high-quality Belt and Road cooperation. Numerous major diplomatic events have highlighted the importance of advancing international vocational education through initiatives such as the Luban Workshop. As a flagship achievement in Sino-foreign cultural exchange, the Luban Workshop is playing an increasingly vital role in deepening friendships between China and its partner countries.

1   Strengthening Global Intellectual Property Protection

Enhancing legal safeguards and actively upholding brand reputation are vital to the Luban Workshop's brand development. The Luban Workshop must further strengthen legal protections by adopting a multi-layered, multidimensional strategy to reinforce brand management. This ensures consistency and authority in its brand image while steadily boosting its social reputation. The first international Luban Workshop trademark has been successfully registered in the United Kingdom, a significant step in safeguarding the brand's rights globally. China has established 29 overseas Luban Workshops across Asia, Europe, and Africa, where brand protection requirements vary by country. To fully secure its legal rights, there is an urgent need to accelerate trademark applications both domestically and internationally. This will enable the Luban Workshop to gain comprehensive intellectual property protection in host countries. Such efforts help maintain market order for the global Luban Workshop initiative, protect the interests of all participating parties, and promote its sustained development, enhancing the Luban Workshop's brand image and public credibility.

2   Improving the Internal Management Mechanism

International cooperation in vocational education faces numerous uncertainties. There is an urgent need to establish a robust project operation and management system. This involves strengthening collaborative management among all participating parties and building a shared governance and operational framework for the Luban Workshop. Through standardized multi-party cooperation agreements, charters, teaching documents, and regulations for laboratories and practical training facilities, the rights and obligations of participants, as well as the practical requirements for degree education and external training, can be clearly defined. Such measures ensure that the Luban Workshop operates in a more scientific and standardized manner, guarantee that key elements like development goals, organizational operations, and resource allocation strictly align with the initiative's core principles, drive high-quality, sustainable progress in areas such as professional education, school-enterprise collaboration, and cultural exchange, thereby achieving consistency in the brand's intrinsic value.

3   Perfecting the Project Quality Assessment System

The Luban Workshop Construction Guidelines clearly stipulate that the initiative operates under a project-based management system, with each project cycle spanning three years. In 2022, during the inaugural World Vocational and Technical Education Development Conference, the first batch of Luban Workshops worldwide received operational certification, witnessed by ambassadors from multiple countries, marking the start of the construction cycle for 22 Luban Workshops. A key challenge is determining how to scientifically evaluate construction quality after three years have passed. This evaluation aims to promote development and improvements through assessment and to integrate assessment with construction. Ensuring the high-quality development of these projects requires systematic scientific research and practical exploration.

The Tianjin Luban Workshop Research and Promotion Center began scientific research and experiments for the pilot evaluation of the Luban Workshops in 2021. This work considers factors such as the socioeconomic development levels of host countries and the characteristics of partner institutions. Over three years, pilot assessments of eight projects have led to the preliminary development of a comprehensive and systematic quality evaluation framework and mechanism.It is recommended that the Luban Workshop Construction Alliance take the experience of Tianjin as a foundation. By widely gathering input from experts, scholars, and all participating parties, the alliance can refine the evaluation metrics, streamline the assessment process, and establish a quality evaluation system that is scientific, objective, and fair. This system could then be applied across all Luban Workshops globally. Additionally, a corresponding management system should be established. First, this includes conducting process inspections and outcome evaluations. The expert panel conducts a comprehensive and objective evaluation of the Luban Workshop's construction process and operational effectiveness, assisting the project team in summarizing experiences, identifying issues, and clarifying directions for subsequent improvements. Second, strict management protocols are essential. At the end of a project's three-year cycle, those meeting quality assurance standards can proceed to the next cycle. Projects falling short must undergo rectification within a specified timeframe as required.

4　Enhancing Empirical Scientific Research

The Luban Workshop initiative has developed in tandem with scientific research since its inception. On one hand, extensive exploratory practices offer valuable lessons for the project's growth. On the other hand, systematic research provides intellectual support and scientific guidance for its development. The Tianjin Luban Workshop Research and Promotion Center has published the annual Luban Workshop Construction and Development Report and the bilingual Overview of Luban Workshop Construction and Development (Chinese-English Edition) [also known as the Luban Workshop Development Bluebook (Chinese-English Edition)] for three consecutive years. These publications employ methods such as surveys and interviews with teachers and students to thoroughly analyze and document the current state and achievements of the Luban Workshop, providing a reference for all participating parties.

Looking ahead, empirical research on overseas projects should be further strengthened. Comprehensive surveys are needed of schools, teachers, students, partner companies, government agencies, and social organizations from both Chinese and foreign sides. By considering the unique contexts of Luban Workshops in various countries, researchers can identify commonalities and distinct characteristics. This involves an in-depth analysis of aspects such as project models, talent cultivation, school-enterprise cooperation, and cultural exchange. The goal is to summarize successful experiences, pinpoint existing issues, analyze limiting factors, and propose reform strategies. These efforts will provide a scientific foundation for the sustainable, high-quality development of the Luban Workshop.

—